TWAYNE'S WORLD AUTHORS SERIES

A Survey of the World's Literature

Sylvia E. Bowman, Indiana University

GENERAL EDITOR

ROMANIA

Eric D. Tappe, University of London

EDITOR

Vasile Alecsandri

(TWAS 204)

TWAYNE'S WORLD AUTHORS SERIES (TWAS)

The purpose of TWAS is to survey the major writers—novelists, dramatists, historians, poets, philosophers, and critics—of the nations of the world. Among the national literatures covered are those of Australia, Canada, China, Eastern Europe, France, Germany, Greece, India, Italy, Japan, Latin America, The Netherlands, New Zealand, Poland, Russia, Scandinavia, Spain, and the African nations, as well as Hebrew, Yiddish, and Latin Classical literatures. This survey is complemented by Twayne's United States Authors Series and English Authors Series.

The intent of each volume in these series is to present a critical-analytical study of the works of the writer; to include biographical and historical material that may be necessary for understanding, appreciation, and critical appraisal of the writer; and to present all material in clear, concise English—but not to vitiate the scholarly content of the work by doing so.

Vasile Alecsandri

By ALEXANDRE CIORANESCU
University of La Laguna

Twayne Publishers, Inc.　：：　New York

Editor's Note

Professor Cioranescu's text was written in Rumanian. It was translated into English by Miss Maria Golescu and revised by me.

E. D. TAPPE

Preface

Vasile Alecsandri is not what one would call a controversial author. His literary destiny is much simpler: during his lifetime his rule over the Rumanian literary world was never contested; but almost continuously from his last years, he has experienced a growing depreciation. His present position is strange. There are many studies and researches of all sorts concerning his biography and his works; the place he occupies in the history of literature is very important; in the last few years editions of his writings have actually multiplied, especially those of his poetry. Yet, on the other side of the balance, criticism has been negative; it has been either nonexistent or conspicuous for its harshness.

This position is not altogether surprising: Alecsandri is forfeiting posthumous glory in payment for the halo he enjoyed during his life. The charges that are brought against him today do not differ from those brought in the past: he is accused, as he was in Macedonski's attacks, of having had too happy a temperament, and, in consequence, of being superficial. Literary sovereignty soon becomes intolerable to the reading public and is posthumously inconceivable. Reaction and disaffection were thus to be expected; but the judgments to which they lead are not more valid than those they combat. Anyone who reads, for instance, the article devoted to Alecsandri in the *History of Rumanian Literature* by G. Călinescu, might almost suppose that this article was not written because it was deserved but for the sheer joy of destruction.

Undoubtedly, Alecsandri does not deserve either of these excesses. The present study is an attempt to deliver an objective judgment, which the distance of a century should render possible. Clearly its general character does not allow us to probe each separate work in depth; we can only endeavor to suggest in broad and simplified lines the moral and literary portrait of a writer.

This portrait has, in Alecsandri's case as in that of all men who have led a public life and have spent themselves in the demand for immediate action, a close connection with their biography. It has therefore been necessary to devote attention to the latter; but even in the strictly biographical chapters, we have striven to give priority to the literary and interior biography and to lay somewhat less stress on his public life and political activity. As this last aspect of his biography is displayed in historical circumstances of which the literary specialist may perhaps be ignorant, but which are nevertheless closely connected with Alecsandri's activity, we have mentioned facts of general interest regarding Rumanian history of his period in the framework of the Chronology which follows.

On the other hand, the quite relative and secondary interest we accord in these pages to his biography, and the fact that the latter merely repeat well-known details, has permitted us to reduce notes and bibliographical references to the minimum. These have been indicated in the Selected Bibliography; in the notes, we have included only less important information, supplementary documentation, and arguments that seem to support some as yet controversial points.

Contents

Chronology

1819
or
1821 July 21, birth of Vasile Alecsandri.

1828 March, pupil at Cuénim's French school at Jassy.

1834 July, goes to study in Paris, where he stays till 1839.

1839 August 31, director of the Pensions Department.

1840 March, meets Elena Negri at Pribeşti. May 15, codirector of the Jassy Theater. November 18, premiere of *Farmazonul din Hîrlău* (The Freemason of Hîrlău).

1842 February 2, his mother dies. Visit to Vienna. May, gives up theater directorship.

1844 January 2, editor of the journal *Propăşirea* (Progress).

1846 April 12, resigns from Pensions Department. June 19, sets off for Constantinople, Brussa, Smyrna. September 5, meets Elena Negri at Trieste, and with her visits Venice, Paris, and Palermo.

1847 May 4, death of Elena Negri on steamer in Bosporus.

1848 March 28, revolutionary manifesto of thirty-five points at Jassy.

1848–
1849 April–December, in exile: Transylvania, Bucovina, Paris, Turkey, Paris.

1850 February 3, director of State Archives at Jassy.

1852 March, his new journal, *România literară* (Literary Rumania), suppressed before first issue distributed. April, *Poesii populare* (Popular Poems), vol. I.

1852–
1853 September–September, travels abroad (after meeting N. Bălcescu at Galatz): Paris, Spain, Morocco, London. June, *Les Doinas,* Paris. July, *Doine şi lăcrămioare* (Doinas and Lilies of the Valley), Paris.

1854–
1855 December 15–July 8, director of Jassy Theater.

1855 January–December, *România literară* restarted, but again suppressed.

1857 April, goes to Bucharest with Moldavian delegation of protest to Danube Commission. October 4, deputy to Assembly (Divan Ad Hoc). November 4, minister of foreign affairs for Moldavia.

1859 January 15, renounces candidacy for throne of Moldavia. February–July, diplomatic mission to Paris, London, Turin. October 23, minister of foreign affairs for Wallachia also.

1860 May, change of government; he retires to Mirceşti.

1861–
1862   March–September, second diplomatic mission: Paris and Turin

1863–
1864   November–May, third diplomatic mission: Paris.

1867   June 2, member of Academic Society of Bucharest (later Rumanian Academy).

1869   May, president of Chamber of Deputies.

1874   February, premiere of *Boieri şi ciocoi* (Nobles and Upstarts).

1875–
1876   Publication of *Opere complete* (Complete Works).

1878   May 22, awarded prize at Montpellier. June 3, fêted at Bucharest.

1879   September 30, premiere of *Despot Vodă* (Prince Despot).

1881   Awarded Năsturel prize by Rumanian Academy.

1883   March 23, reading of *Fîntîna Blanduziei* (The Fountain of Bandusia) at Bucharest.

1884   March 22, premiere of *Fintina Blanduziei.*

1885   March 9, premiere of *Ovidiu* (Ovid).

1885–
1890   April–June, minister plenipotentiary at Paris with annual holidays at Mirceşti.

1890   August 22, dies at Mirceşti.

CHAPTER 1

Time of Illusions

IN spite of repeated attempts to elucidate it, the exact date of Vasile Alecsandri's birth remains hypothetical. The day and month seem to be July 21; as to the year, it is difficult to choose between 1819 and 1821. Both dates are mentioned by the poet himself, who in his turn may have had to rely on guesswork.[1] In the absence of a convincing document, we will merely say that the poet preferred to appear younger, with the result that the date 1821 is more frequently attested, while that of 1819 seems more acceptable.

His father, Vasile Alexandri—the spelling "Alecsandri" was an innovation of the poet's—was born about 1793, received some education in Greek and entered the Moldavian administration, in which he rose to the highest posts to which he could have aspired. At the same time he did much business of his own, especially in the export of cereals. He ended by possessing six large landed estates and two houses in Jassy. He married Elena Cozoni, the daughter of Greeks who had recently become Rumanized.

The poet's childhood was spent in the Jassy home of his parents. As was then customary in boyar families, the child grew up mostly among the slaves and servants. He remembered them tenderly and with a kind of gratitude for having guided his first steps: mother Gahița, who nursed and brought him up; her husband, Gheorghe Ciolacu the manager, who taught him Greek; Didică the Gypsy fiddler, from whom he heard the first popular songs, later jotting down some compositions from his repertory; Vasile Porojan the Gypsy boy who had been his playmate and partner in childish adventures and who, as slave, received all the punishment for "the little master's" follies.

From 1828, the year his father bought the estate of Mircești in the Siret valley, the poet spent all his summers in the old manor house of that village, to which he remained attached throughout his life. The boy thus developed in ease and liberty in a family in which he lacked nothing except perhaps a touch of severity, a family more attached to its slaves than to distant relatives; in a paternalist universe which, for his tender age, excluded worrying questions and uncertain prospects; in a natural setting characterized by the bland sweetness of the soft Moldavian landscape, set midway between flatland and ravines.

It would be possible, for instance, to claim—and it has sometimes actually been claimed—that Alecsandri found his first stimulus toward folklore in the Gypsy Didică's songs, and that, by causing him to appreciate popular poetry at such an early age, the fiddler of his childhood determined his vocation as a collector. It is easily said; but it is equally true that this vocation manifested itself much later, as a kind of return to the sources, and precisely when the poet, after having emerged from a first phase of alienation, came back to folklore under the influence of illustrious examples and after mature consideration. Probably he would never have ventured to collect and publish popular ballads relying just on the strength of Didică the Gypsy and his own appreciation: in order to make a decision, he needed the stimulus of an example and of a model.

However this may be, it was during these years that the poet began his studies, studies that are as free as everything he did in life. It was probably Gheorghe, his first teacher, who gave him his first Greek text, a vernacular translation of *Le Magasin des Enfants* by Madame Le Prince de Beaumont, better known for her tale entitled *La Belle et la Bête*. About 1827, when he was six (if not eight), a family tutor was brought into the house—a monk from Maramureş, Gherman Vida, an amateur devoted to history—who probably gave him elementary instruction as well as instruction in Greek and French. The following year he entered the French boarding school which Victor Cuénim, an ex-officer of Napoleon's Grand Army who had probably been left behind in Russia as a prisoner, was just then opening in Jassy. The program of studies, spread out over six years, was more or less an equivalent of the program in force in the French lycées, with Rumanian and German courses in addition; but Alecsandri himself confesses that the German had been of no use to him.

In the summer of 1834, he was sent to continue his studies in Paris, together with three other sons of boyars, one of whom was Alexandru Cuza, the future prince. After a preparatory year with Professor Cotte, he passed his baccalaureate on October 27, 1835.

In the following academic year (1835–36) he studied medicine, but in the end he could not bear the stark reality of the operating theaters, and, taking advantage of one of his father's visits to Paris, he persuaded him that the profession of doctor was not the most appropriate one for the son of a boyar. He therefore switched to law (1836–37), which again he endured only for one year; after that, he thought of trying the profession of engineer. But for the latter he required a certificate of scientific studies, in which he failed, so he was saved a year of engineering, which would certainly have led him to a result similar to his medical and legal studies.

Learning meant constraint, steadfastness, and, in great measure, stubbornness—and the young student had not deceived his father in explaining to him that those were qualities he did not possess. Otherwise, he was intelligent, and his secondary studies had been well accomplished; he was curious and liked reading. In his short progress through the faculties of medicine and law he had not wasted his time but had worked seriously and had passed some examinations. But he evaded sustained effort and constraint all the more cheerfully because his family's affluence and his father's good nature allowed it. His father admired him and was pleasantly surprised and easily won over by the brilliant levity and the charming presence and conversation of the young man, who had become a perfect Parisian.

Consequently, Alecsandri's academic failure should not be interpreted in terms of deficiency or incompetence but simply as an idiosyncrasy of temperament. Medicine did not appeal to him because he was interested in something else. He had switched from one study to another without being false to literature; and it is odd that among the many careers he considered he did not for one moment think of Letters.

It is true that this subject was not considered a career, and it is also true that for literature he needed no diploma. He was a tireless reader and, either in school or out of it, he perfectly assimilated French literature. We know from his own statements that his idols during those years were Chateaubriand, whom he read on his way back from medical lectures, and Rousseau and Lamartine, whom he had discovered when reading law. These contemporary readings were grafted onto a stock of classical and post-classical formation and are fundamental for the understanding of Alecsandri's literary career.

His other studies left slight traces on his development. As a Latinist he passed his certificate with a satisfactory grade, but his

knowledge was poor. There is no doubt that he knew Greek well
enough to keep up an ordinary conversation or to act as an interpreter if need be.[2] But it was modern Greek, and he made use of it
only to distort and modulate it in a comic way; we have no proof
that he read the Greek classics at all. On the other hand, French
authors were as familiar to him as they were to any Frenchman of
his time; they were, so to say, his own classics, the authors under
whose shadow he developed and with whom he claimed to compete.

In order to understand how far his integration into this atmosphere went, it suffices to examine his French correspondence
when he carries on a dialogue with one whom he is sure will understand his allusions: for instance, with his old friend of student
days, Ion Ghica. All his expressions become transparent, the
style becomes an ingenious play between what he has to say and what
others have said before him; and literary reminiscences spontaneously blossom under his pen.[3] The world of his associations of
ideas is that of French classicism. His living models end, it is true,
with Lamartine and Victor Hugo, but Racine, Voltaire, Delille,
Parny, are not less alive for him.

In the spring of 1839, Alecsandri's parents decided that it was
time for him to come home. He returned by way of Italy, where he
was met by his friends Costache Negri and Nicolae Docan, and
together they followed the standard itinerary, from Livorno through
Florence to Rome, and back through Bologna, Padua, and Venice.
From that moment, Italy remained one of his greatest attachments.

The young man, now twenty years old, who came back to Jassy
toward the end of the summer of 1839, was truly Frenchified, not
only because he wore clothes after the latest Parisian fashion and
sported ties bought in Italy, but also because he probably could
not write Rumanian properly. He had been educated in foreign
languages only. In Paris he had actually begun to write verses, in
French, as might be expected; and so he continued after his return
to Jassy, with some compositions that have been published and
which must date back to 1840, if they are not rewritings of older
Parisian themes.[4] Up to that date, as far as we know, the idea of
becoming a Rumanian writer does not seem to have crossed his
mind.

Nonetheless, this young man had not become a foreigner and did
not need a long period of adaptation in order to be once more in
tune with a world so different from the one he had left. Perhaps

Jassy life, with its cosmopolitan society, its French theater, its drawing rooms where conversations were carried on in French, did not feel like a place of exile; it may also be that the family ties were too strong for the prodigal son to be a stranger in his own home.[5] Or perhaps, the poet had been impatiently awaiting to return to the country he loved. For such was his unstable temperament: whenever he was in Jassy or at Mircești, he dreamt of sunny shores and exotic landscapes; whenever he went away, homesickness gnawed at his heart.

However that may be, Jassy life took possession of him without delay. He was appointed head of the Department of Pensions in the Moldavian Ministry of Finance (August 31, 1839), owing apparently to the influence of his father, who was the chief official in that ministry at the time. The drawing rooms of Jassy opened their doors to this distinguished young man of good social standing with a Parisian halo, and a flair for brisk and entertaining conversation. It was probably due to the charm of his traveler's tales that Mihail Kogălniceanu, who had studied with him under Gherman Vida, immediately invited him to write something in Rumanian for the review he was preparing under the title of *Dacia literară* (Literary Dacia).

Kogălniceanu's personality was not only strong, it was demanding: he had experience as a writer and was equipped with both a literary program and the wish to have the nascent Rumanian literature based on national traditions and not on foreign imitations. Alecsandri yielded to the temptation offered by his old fellow student and gave him *Buchetiera de la Florența* (The Flower Girl of Florence), though not too willingly; for in order to make Alecsandri keep his promise, Kogălniceanu had to kidnap him and isolate him in his country place at Rîpile.

Meanwhile, with Kogălniceanu and Costache Negruzzi, Alecsandri collaborated in other ways as well. On March 18, 1840, they received from the Moldavian government a collective concession that made them directors of the National Theater for the term of four years, under the obligation of staging one hundred plays, twenty-five of which were to be original. It was the first organized attempt to make the Rumanian theater a permanent institution, and from Alecsandri's point of view, it was decisive as to his later propensities.

Alecsandri seems to have traveled much in the year 1840. In

March he was at Pribeşti, the estate of Vasile Rosetti, a brother-in-law of his old friend Costache Negri, with whom he had traveled through Italy the year before; on the same occasion he made the acquaintance of the latter's sister, Elena Negri, married to one of the Vîrnav-Liteanus, who was to play such an important part in his emotional life. It was probably in April that the stay at Kogăl-niceanu's country house mentioned above took place. July found him in Fălticeni and December in Botoşani; it is between these two dates that we must place an excursion into the mountains about which we have but scanty details.

Back in Jassy, the writer took his new obligations as a theater director more seriously than those as chief of the Pensions Department. During this year he composed two comedies, *Farmazonul din Hîrlău* (The Freemason of Hîrlău) (November, 1840) and *Cinovnicul şi modista* (The Civil Servant and the Milliner) (February 5, 1841) which were not printed and the text of which have not reached us; they were mere imitations and adaptations of French works, in which the intention was more promising than the result.

His first journey to Bucharest is to be placed in 1841 and so are the French verses that were his contribution to *Spicuitorul moldo-valah* (The Moldo-Wallachian Gleaner), the more or less official review edited by Gheorghe Asaki. He was promoted to the rank of *spătar* (sword-bearer) on June 2, 1841. The following February 3, the poet lost his mother, Elena Alexandri, who could not have been more than forty-two. Her death was a severe shock to Alec-sandri's father, then traveling abroad; the son was obliged to go to Vienna and find his father the necessary treatment before bringing him home.

The years that followed were decisive in Alecsandri's life. Up to that date the young aristocrat had behaved, both in life and in literature as a mere dilettante. Suddenly, from about 1843, the literary destiny of Alecsandri appeared to be fixed once and for all. The writer renounced French as a medium of artistic expression and started to write verses in Rumanian.[6] These are verses of a certain style and inspiration—very original and easy to recognize, in which the half-bucolic, half-heroic atmosphere of post-classicism, tinted by the pageantry of Ossian's heroes and the sighs of Parny— dons a peasant garb and claims to be the expression of popular and historical sentiment, the translation of Rumanian landscape and ethos. With slight variations of intention and with more evident differences in key, this remained, forever crystallized, the poetical art of Alecsandri.

This poetic universe was not a revealed truth nor did it spring suddenly like Minerva from her father's head into the young poet's imagination. Its component elements are, of course, multiple and often escape detection. But it is evident that there is no question of any revolutionary or surprising ideal. Here as everywhere Alecsandri did not swim against the current, but made use of it without letting himself be drawn further than he thought fit. His classical education prevented him from becoming a pathfinder through unknown places, but it showed him clearly the importance of adapting to his own use paths indicated by others.

Perhaps his own temperament combined with his initial education and the general trends of European pre-Romanticism to indicate a path of tranquillity. Alecsandri as a poet breathed freely in the atmosphere of the troubadour genre, with all its shades of epic languor, with its obvious preference for erotic-heroic inspiration, with its sham Arcadia and its lyrical and eloquent shepherds, with its neat and delicate landscapes like a tapestry, with its personages glossy as precious china who, clothing and sentiments alike, seem surprised and immobilized in an endless Sunday.

As to the idea of replacing the Sèvres vase and the Aubusson tapestry by a rustic rug and by a small wooden pail decorated with carving of ornamental flowers, the credit belongs to Alecsandri even if he did not originate the idea. This idea was in the air during that period. Kogălniceanu had given it expression and had transformed it into a program of activity in *Dacia literară*, a program which the poet had had made his own in all points. His good friend Ion Ghica directed his attention toward the same horizons in 1842 when, accompanied by the Wallachian poet Grigore Alexandrescu, they went for a trip to the mountains around the Olt River with the intention of reliving on the spot the glories of Rumanian history. In short, the literary formula advocated and practiced by Alecsandri coincided by its double objective—modern form and traditional background—with all the aspirations and programs of the reforming youth to which he belonged by age, education, and convictions.

In this way, Alecsandri was led toward an artistic formula which he himself called true Rumanian poetry[7]. In practice, the poet meant it as an alliance between popular themes and the refined versification of cultivated lyric fostered by foreign influence. This accounts for the double orientation of his poetical preoccupations throughout these years: toward the popular vein and toward personal inspiration.

Popular poetry drew his attention yet again between 1842 and 1844 when, for reasons of health, during summertime he had to go repeatedly to the mountains; one of these trips was humorously described in the prose sketch *O primblare la munți* (A Trip in the Mountains). It was apparently about this time that he took to systematically noting down the products of the popular muse which he had occasion to hear, thus gradually assembling a voluminous collection, of which he did not publish anything before 1849, but which by that date was already fairly complete.

Judging by the elements at our disposal, it would be difficult to maintain that Alecsandri had deliberately transformed himself into a folklorist and that from the very beginning his intention had been to publish the results of his literary research in a volume. It is true that he did so, but the thought of such a publication came to him much later, after the collection was completed. Consequently, he must have begun it with a different purpose. Perhaps the materials thus collected were, according to his original purpose, to have constituted a kind of personal documentation, mere raw material meant to be used, interpreted, and transformed by the poet according to the artistic canon mentioned above. In any case, the considerable bulk of the collected popular poems indicates a sustained effort and a relatively large number of spontaneous collaborators: it is therefore evident that there can be no question of the mere curiosity of an intellectual but of a veritable campaign persistently conducted for a number of years. This is the more surprising in that the duration and continuity of this effort are just the sacrifices which Alecsandri was least disposed to make. Of all his works, literary or otherwise, the collection of popular poems is that which cost him most effort: it is therefore easy to deduce that the importance he attributed to it must have been particularly great and worth the price paid for it.

At the same time, Alecsandri was publishing his first Rumanian poems. It is significant that the first one appeared in *Calendarul pentru poporul românesc pe anul 1843* (The Rumanian People's Calendar for 1843), the editor and publisher of which was Kogălniceanu; it was, consequently, under the aegis of the same friend who had urged him on the path of national inspiration and under whose ascendancy the poet would continue to find himself until much later. In all these verses one finds the association of effects to which we have already drawn attention, that is, the use of popular themes and rhythms to sing of pre-Romantic inspirations and sentiments.

At the outset of his poetical career, Alecsandri proceeded like a musical composer using a popular theme; the work of imagination was sometimes limited to mere comment, as in *Cîntec haiducesc* (Outlaw Song), or at other times risked original modulations and new effects, as in *Groza*.

Most of the poem that would later make up his first collection of verse belong to the years 1842 and 1843. As a man used to frequenting drawing rooms, the author first read them aloud to his friends, especially in the house of Alecu Balş.[8] It was natural that the reaction of the first auditors should be one of uneasy surprise. Lyrical poetry familiar to them, that of Conachi, expressed somewhat similar sentiments, but in the languorous and faded forms of fiddlers' songs: the rustic pitch, lively and in some measure aggressive, of Alecsandri's lyricism seemed to them on a lower level and constituted to their unaccustomed ears a vulgarity made even more shocking by novelty. Yet his true friends recognized from the very beginning a needed process of purification in his purpose and encouraged him in his efforts. According to his own confession, the most precious and understanding prompting had come to him from Elena Negri—she was both muse and admirer.

Carried away by the whirlwind of literary activity, Alecsandri once more joined with Kogălniceanu and Ion Ghica in order to publish with them in Jassy a new literary review meant to replace *Dacia literară,* which had only too rapidly disappeared. It was to be called *Propăşirea* (Progress), but this title was suppressed by the government as subversive, so that the review appeared under the innocent title of *Foaie ştiinţifică şi literară* (Scientific and Literary Paper). The review did not last even one year, being suppressed by the autocratic government of Mihai Sturdza, who was disturbed by any independent activity, especially when it failed to harmonize with his Russophile politics. Kogălniceanu was restricted to house detention, and Alecsandri would have undergone the same had it not been for the intervention and influence of his father, who was one of the prince's men of affairs and was in favor at court. The short-lived *Propăşirea* is nonetheless of considerable importance to the history of Rumanian literature. The credit of having recruited collaborators from all areas inhabited by Rumanians seems to belong to Alecsandri, who contributed eight poems and as many pieces in prose. To Alecsandri also goes the credit of having for the first time brought together in the pages of the same publication the most illustrious literary names of his time, beginning with Nicolae Bălcescu, Grigore Alexandrescu, and D. Bolintineanu.

It was about this same time that our writer turned to the stage again, giving Jassy the comedy *Iorgu de la Sadagura* (Iorgu of Sadagura), presented for the first time on January 23, 1844. It was his first original play and the first great success of the Rumanian stage. The date is a memorable one in the annals of that stage history, and contemporaries felt it to be so.

In the following years, the poet continued writing for the theater. This insistence is not to be explained only by his legitimate desire to take advantage of the resounding success of his *Iorgu de la Sadagura* but more because he realized that in the specific circumstances of the period the stage was an ampler and more efficient platform than books and journals. He presented one play after another in Jassy: *Spătarul Haţmaţuchi* (Swordbearer Haţmaţuchi), a one-act comedy (1844); *Rămăşagul* (The Wager), a kind of cross between vaudeville and the dramatic proverbs of Musset; and lastly *Iaşii in carnaval* (Carnival at Jassy), his second big success (December 22, 1845). This time, the success was largely due to its mockery of the Moldavian government's obsession with conspiracy.

In real life, the young reformers—to which group Alecsandri belonged (like most intellectuals trained in the West)—were not content with making fun of the government. Crushed between three great empires—of Turkey, Russia, and Austro-Hungary—the Rumanian principalities had for over a century been unable to lead an independent political life. The dignity and integrity of the state, the independence of its representatives, the objective and disinterested justice and administration were nothing but hollow words at a time when in the whole of Europe public life itself was changing at a dizzy speed. It was evident that reform could not be imposed from the inside but inevitably depended on the international conjuncture that had brought about such a state of affairs and on the diminishing of the intolerable pressure exerted by the undesired Russian protectorate.

Waiting for the decisive hour to strike without being able to speed it, the young patriots who believed that their country had still its historic role to play tried to form a group and prepare themselves. One of the most important points of the national program was the union of the two principalities, Wallachia and Moldavia. The future leaders of the two countries established contacts, at the heart of which was Costache Negri, not only because of his outstanding personality but also because his estate of Mînjina was situated near the border.[9] It was there that even before 1848 Alecsandri, Kogălniceanu, Negruzzi, Alecu Russo, and C. Rolla—all Moldavians—more than once came together with Wallachians, such as Ion Ghica, Nicolae Bălcescu, or Constantin Filipescu. It was there that Alecsandri formed a close and lasting friendship with the great historian Bălcescu, and it was there that many reforms actually accomplished in the following years were debated and designed. Most important of all, it was there that a unity of purpose was achieved that rendered possible—without problems and without a major crisis—the union of 1859 and, after that, the fusion of both governments and also of the two administrations. Apart from the important role he played at the center of the National party, Alecsandri was attracted to Mînjina more often than the other leaders of political life because of his love for Elena Negri, whom he had known since 1840 and who—separated from her husband in 1843—used to spend the summer in the nearby estate of Blînzi in the district of Tecuci.

In August and September, 1845, the poet was on a journey to Constantinople which was followed by another to Bucharest in January, 1846; we do not know, however, if he pursued political aims or if he had been called there by other interests. In any case, his too frequent absence, together with his genuine dislike for routine, compelled him to resign from the office of chief of the Pensions Department on March 29, 1846. This decision may have been brought about by the prospect of a lengthy absence from the country secretly planned with Elena Negri just about that time.

The delicate health of Elena, who suffered from consumption, drove her to seek a milder sky and more constant treatment. The two lovers had earlier agreed on a common program, which called for a long absence with departures in directions apparently quite different and a meeting abroad, far from the spiteful eyes of acquaintances and the gossip unavoidable on such occasions. Elena left Jassy sometime in May, 1846 with the purpose of consulting physicians in Vienna; afterward, she went on to the spa of Ems and finally met Alecsandri on September 5, in Trieste. Alecsandri had announced an intended journey to the East, for which he had obtained a passport, but he had chosen this opposite direction in order to mislead acquaintances. Starting in June, he spent two months in Constantinople, which he already knew from the previous year. After trips in various directions, to Brussa and Athens, he hastened to Trieste where Elena herself arrived at the prearranged date.

This is the beginning of the poet's great idyll, followed by a tragic aftermath that endured seven months and proved to be the most distressing period of his life. Settled in Venice at the Benzoni Palace on the Grand Canal their existence was for two months that of two perfect romantic lovers. For those all-too-short days, we possess a notebook with daily entries in French, which is incontestably the supreme masterpiece of his life; and this is to be expected, for this young man, lucid and critical, but at the same time deeply in love with life, merely confesses his surprise and happiness without literary self-consciousness.

But soon the Venetian climate became too harsh for Elena. They were obliged to start on a long and fatiguing journey through Trieste and Graz to Salzburg and Munich, then to Strassburg and Paris and at last through Marseilles, Genoa, and Livorno and on to Naples, in search of sun and an ever receding health. From January to March, 1847, they stayed in Palermo, together with Nicolae Bălcescu, the friend and confidant of them both. Elena still entertained some illusions as to her state of health; short remissions led them to believe that danger was averted, and the three friends spent their evenings in writing (it is on this occasion that Alecsandri wrote *Piatra din casă* (The Stone in the House), to amuse Elena, reading aloud what they had written and discussing literature.

But the catastrophe grew nearer, and the poet decided to return to Moldavia in spite of all the risk a journey together might involve—proof that the health of the patient was definitely compromised and that the world's gossip no longer mattered. In fact, Alecsandri returned to Jassy alone: Elena Negri had died on the boat as it entered the Golden Horn on May 4, 1847, and was buried in Constantinople. From the greatest adventure of his life, the poet returned empty-handed, with a hidden wound, which to his last hour would not cease to bleed.

CHAPTER 2

Between Action and Poetry

A FTER the death of Elena Negri, and after what we shall call a period of readaptation, Alecsandri was more and more caught up by the political whirl. His high position among intellectual and progressive youth marked him out naturally as one of the representatives of national emancipation. From 1848 to 1878 Rumanian political life passed through a period of essential changes; it was thus natural that the poet should have intensely lived this epoch of great reforms in which he played a part. Alecsandri was what we would today call an engaged writer.

His contribution to the history of the union of the two principalities is at least as important as that of Kogălniceanu, for example, or that of Negri and other promoters of the national unionist idea. If one adds that Alecsandri also had the leading role of poet of the national renascence and in this connection enjoyed undeniable popularity—infinitely greater than that of many men exclusively dedicated to political action—it may be asserted without exaggeration that he played by far the most important part in the making of the union and that he conducted himself with dignity, understanding, and efficiency. Yet the poet did not want (or did not know how) to benefit by the popularity thus won nor by his undeniable merits, and he abandoned the fight before having ended it. His political career led him to the highest offices, to play a predominant part in the Moldavian ministry and afterward in the Wallachian one, and even brought him at a certain moment almost to the steps of the princely throne. Yet each time he took a step backward, a step as decisive as the one that he had taken forward. In the end, he retired completely from public life, voluntarily abandoning the splendid cards he might have played.

It is difficult to determine the actual cause of this growing disaffection. A special circumstance is perhaps to be taken into consideration: outward successes were accompanied by much secret suffering. Political action is not for emotional people, and Alecsandri was impenitently emotional; he was a believer in the virtues of friendship, in the idyllic beauty of realities, in the excellence of social life. Like Rousseau, he constantly suffered because of the gulf between his humanitarian conceptions, social or nationalistic, and the results to which they led in reality. Like most creators of systems and fictions, he undoubtedly loved his fellow human beings —as an idea. At every encounter with men as they really were, he expected too much from them and received too little: he could only feel deceived and in a certain measure betrayed. Ever ready to give of himself to all comers, he suffered from this generosity. In the end, he retired into himself to avoid further giving. The fact is that all of life's experiences hurt him. To understand this excessive sensitivity, one must bear in mind Alecsandri's own constitution: physically he possessed the same exaggerated and morbid sensibility that we discover in his mind. The cruel disappointment in Italy must also be taken into account. On this as on many other occasions, life showed him the same smiling malice, giving with one hand what it took with the other.

What we have called the period of readaptation was short. Back in Moldavia after having left his youth interred in the cemetery of Pera in Constantinople, the poet began to shun the world and his acquaintances. He concealed grief with the utmost tact— according to some biographers, with a lack of sensibility that proved him incapable of deep feeling. His love for Elena was a secret shared by very few friends. Finally, as his health had been in some measure impaired[1] by those last months of fearful waiting, he removed himself in the summer of 1847 from the society of his Jassy acquaintances in order to go to the spa of Balta Albă and then to that of Mehadia. Balta Albă, not far from the town of Brăila, eastern Wallachia, was at that moment a fashionable spa because of the healing virtues of the neighboring lake. The discovery of these virtues was still of a very recent date, and the watering place had not yet changed its primitive aspect of a Godforsaken village where, in season, hundreds of guests packed as best they could into small houses wholly lacking in comfort. The sight of a refined society on holiday in picturesque discomfort did not fail to attract the notice of the poet who described it in one of his pleasantest prose pieces, *Balta Albă*. Proof that his state of mind did not prevent him from noting with attentive curiosity what was happening around him or even from making fun of himself and the others!

Besides, even if he wished to flee from people, it is probable that people did not flee from him, and Balta Albă in mid-season did not look in the least like a hermitage. It is there that young Alexandru Odobescu, then a stripling, met him; from this we deduce that the poet did not live in retirement, but took part in social life and enjoyed friendships and conversation. Owing to all this he was able to hide his deep wound in such a way that the majority of his biographers have not even sensed it; in fact, they have refused to believe it could exist in a man who returned so soon to frivolous amusements. Odobescu remembered having seen him at Balta Albă gay and unanimously admired by a society set on having a good time. For us who know where he had come from, such a statement unintentionally takes on the aspect of a reproach. But the poet did not bear with this gaiety for more than a week, and he left for another spa where there would be fewer persons he would know, Mehadia or Băile Herculane in the Banat region. He stayed there two or three weeks for the baths. During his hours of leisure he probably walked about the surrounding mountains, and he may have resumed the researches on folklore he had undertaken in Moldavia some years before.

Alecsandri appeared to be a young aristocrat permanently on holiday. To the few friends who shared his secret, especially to Elena's family and Bălcescu, who had lived through the drama in Palermo with him, he was a man who was struggling to regain his balance and who needed the solicitude and understanding of friendship to find himself again. In these dramatic circumstances, Bălcescu seems to have supported him in the most intelligent and efficient way. Bălcescu, who had remained in the West, surrounded him with proofs of affection and understanding. Above all, he prompted him with the authority of a friend to find an outlet to his grief by rendering himself useful to others, especially to his country. For a man like Alecsandri, who himself admitted that he needed an affectionate mentor, Bălcescu was thus taking the place which Kogălniceanu had occupied; and this second intellectual friendship was at least as decisive as the first. Owing to it, Alecsandri gave in completely to the temptation of politics. For him the subtle alcohol of action was indeed the happiest remedy, and he himself understood that this was the only way to forget Elena without betraying her.[2]

Meanwhile, he did not quite abandon literature. In *Calendarul pentru Români* (The Calendar for Rumanians), which Asaki was publishing with the date 1848, but which appeared in the last months of 1847, he published the prose sketch of Balta Albă mentioned above, together with *Păunaşul Codrilor* (The Forest Peacock), the first poem of his folk collection. On February 3, 1848, a short comedy, *Nuntă ţărănească* (The Peasant Wedding), was produced for the first time. It displayed the rusticity of Alecsandri's new lyrical inspiration. The show was organized for charity and was acted by young people from high society who dressed up in peasant costume. Thus it made its entry into literature and social life—somewhat as the pastoral disguises and beribboned lambs in the Trianon of Marie Antoinette did.

Exactly as at the court of France in the late eighteenth century, the villagers' dance on the stage at Jassy was going on over a volcano which was on the point of eruption. The second presentation of the comedy on March 9, 1848, took place in the presence of a public which was already agitated by the recent news of the revolution that had broken out in Paris and was to spread over the whole of Europe like wildfire. Revolution was expected in the principalities, and all the reformers wished for it even if they were not actually participants in it. In Moldavia the weak and corrupt regime of Mihail Sturdza, extremely unpopular in all classes of society, was maintained solely by the Russian protectorate. But the Moldavian revolution only lasted three days: in fact, it hardly deserves to be called a revolution. All along the initiative seems to have been with the prince, and the course of events, remote controlled by the palace, was a good lesson in Machiavellian policy. Sturdza pretended to listen to the complaints of the people and organized a conference with the chiefs of the active generation. On March 27, a public meeting was called in the presence of the minister of the interior, and a committee of sixteen persons was designated to draft a memoir of complaints without delay.

The committee, of which Alecsandri was one, met next day and drafted a memoir that is known as the Memoir of the Thirty-five Points. The secretary of the committee and author of the memoir seems to have been Alecsandri himself.

Some of the members of the committee presented themselves to the palace with petitions approved by the sixteen and signed by a great number of citizens. The prince attempted some bargaining with regard to a few points, then abruptly dismissed the delegates. On March 29, they were all arrested, each one at his home. Over two hundred persons were thus detained, and the revolution was drowned not in blood but in ridicule. Those who had time or had been warned took refuge in the country. Alecsandri was not immediately arrested, possibly because of the consideration enjoyed by his father. But he had been a member of the committee and author of the unlucky memoir, and consequently it was easy to guess that the initial indulgence was not an oversight but a disguised and friendly incitement to flight. Immediately after these events if not that same night, he made for the mountains and took refuge at Hangu, where the Cantacuzinos, family friends who were in some measure compromised by the part taken by one of them in the same events, had a house and estate. His intention was probably to wait there for developments, so that if it became clear that he must leave the country, he might take advantage of its nearness to the frontiers of Transylvania.

At Hangu he had the opportunity of studying at close quarters the reactions of aristocrats torn between the wish to save their estate and their prestige and the wish to follow their conscience— and deciding to sacrifice the latter. He was also able to study the reaction of the peasants, who were called upon to protect their masters and who, not caring about the fate of the prince or the Jassy aristocracy, did not see further than their immediate wants. The Prince had played his own game; among the so-called reformers, the majority, like the Hangu peasants, sought to further their own interests.

The Cantacuzinos had no difficulty in agreeing with those in power and quickly scattered their guard of improvised protectors. Alecsandri, who was not included either in the proscription lists nor in the negotiated pardons, but was simply ignored, chose the road to exile. About mid-April, 1848 he clandestinely crossed the frontier, guided over the mountains by some peasants. The poet's exile lasted about two years. In May–June, 1848 he stayed in Braşov, where he worked in close connection with the national group of exiled Moldavians and also with Rumanians from Transylvania who were organizing their own national movement. In order to defend patriotic interests and the action that had taken place that March, Alecsandri wrote and published in Braşov a pamphlet bearing the general title *In numele Moldovei, a omenirii şi a lui Dumnezeu* (In the Name of Moldavia, Mankind, and God) and signed it in his capacity as a "member of the committee elected by the people for the drafting of its claims." It is a defense of the Moldavian National party and an indictment of Mihail Sturdza's government, which shows that, although disappointed by the failure of the movement, the poet did not intend to abandon its objectives.

On the other hand, he collaborated actively with the group of Moldavian revolutionaries in connection with a possible attack on Moldavia. On May 24, he also drew up and signed with them a new and openly revolutionary manifesto containing the basic principles of the movement.[3] The program therein developed is much more progressive than the thirty-five points of Jassy and comprises, in six points, a total policy of political, social, and financial liberalization, the abolition of privileges, and the union of the two principalities.

During these months, the Rumanians of Transylvania were actively organizing their own national resistance, the first manifestation of which was the National Assembly at Blaj, intended as an answer to the Hungarian revolutionaries who sought to disengage themselves from the grip of the Austrian Empire without considering the interests of other nationalities inside the empire.

Alecsandri himself felt the importance of these activities. As early as 1844 he had endeavored to gather around *Propăşirea* writers from all the areas inhabited by Rumanians. To this national problem he totally dedicated himself during his stay in Transylvania. Foundations were being so deeply shaken that the realization of hopes hitherto incredible seemed to be possible. In fact, not only he but also other Transylvanian and Moldavian fighters thought that a reconstruction of the old Dacian kingdom might be brought about, an aim sporadically pursued throughout the preceding centuries.

These fresh preoccupations were reflected in his work. From his sojourn in Braşov date his poem *15 Mai 1848* (May, 15, 1848), dedicated to the Blaj Assembly; the hymn *Către Români* (To the Rumanians), which is an open incitement to national revolution, addressed to Rumanians everywhere;[4] *Sentinela română* (The Rumanian Sentry), one of the author's best known poems, an epic glorification of the past[5]; *Motul şi Secuiul* (The Motz and the Szekely); *Hora Ardealului* (The Hora of Transylvania), and other poems that reflect national aspirations.

By the middle of June, 1848, the two Alecsandri brothers (Iancu had recently arrived from Moldavia) and their friend Costache Negri left Braşov for Bucovina, where they hoped to exercise a more direct action on Moldavian public opinion. They were received in Cernăuţi and supported by its Rumanian intellectuals, especially by the Hurmuzachi brothers, and they met other groups of Moldavian exiles with whom they established a revolutionary committee. Alecsandri was its secretary and carried on an active correspondence and drafted all kinds of memoirs and manifestos.

As a result of the success obtained during that summer by the revolutionary movement in Wallachia and the setting up of a provisional government in Bucharest, there followed for the group in Cernăuţi a few months of feverish expectation. In the end it became evident that revolution could not win on its own and that the Russo-Turkish joint effort would soon strangle it. The group of Moldavian refugees adopted a new political idea: national emancipation could not be attained from within, so it was necessary to interest the great powers in bringing about a solution at the European level. The originality of this conception has not been sufficiently stressed.[6] By virtue of it, the refugees in Cernăuţi took upon themselves the task of drawing the attention of the Great Powers to the actual situation. In short, they voluntarily transformed themselves into propagandists of the national idea and scattered in all directions to undertake a new kind of apostleship.

Alecsandri was assigned to Paris. He arrived there in mid-September and closely collaborated with Alexandru Golescu, who had already been sent there by the provisional government of Bucharest with the same task of propaganda. They exploited earlier friendships with Frenchmen, and they got in touch with the editorial staff of most Parisian newspapers and caused the publication of an important series of informative articles, commentaries, and news items regarding the Rumanian lands. Many of these articles were written by Alecsandri himself, of course with the assistance of Golescu and a French friend, Baligot de Beyne, editor of the *Presse d'Orient.* For a whole year in Paris the poet directed an odd kind of press bureau which was neither commercial nor subsidized but was supported mainly by the good will of the editors. The bulk of articles and information they succeeded in spreading throughout the Paris press is astounding. By the new importance it gave to news coming from a part of Europe almost unknown at the time, this press campaign succeeded in forming a current of opinion. The fact that Napoleon III's France permanently advocated the Rumanian cause was not a matter of chance, nor is it sufficiently explained solely by the interest of imperial diplomacy. In this connection, Alecsandri's personal charm played the part which history ascribed to Cleopatra's nose.

At the beginning of the year 1849 interest in these propagandist activities seemed to flag. The Bucharest revolution had been crushed; the question was no longer topical. At the same time, the psychology of exile began to complicate the structure of the refugee group with all kinds of animosities and rivalries. Alecsandri would not confuse the cause he defended with the cause of one single party. In all discussions of the émigrés this is invariably his position. One of these discussions took place in Constantinople and Brussa which he revisited some time in April–July, 1849.

This return to Constantinople, two years after Elena Negri's death, takes on the aspect of a pilgrimage; it is difficult to believe that it had nothing to do with such recent and painful memories. In Paris, another woman had entered Alecsandri's life, the charming Dridri, whose biography he was later to sketch. Marie Angélique Chatâignez was an actress: their tie, however the poet might beautify and idealize it, was only an adventure of the kind customary in the world of the stage. It is therefore probable that this is how the poet himself looked upon it at the start: he was then twenty-eight, and this experience could not be but flattering to him. Yet he was too emotional, in the complete sense of the word, and could not help becoming attached to the young woman who must have been particularly pleasing and sincerely fond of him, nor could he fail to consider this sentiment as a kind of betrayal of Elena's memory. The journey to Constantinople may in a sense have been a pilgrimage of atonement to the still fresh grave at Pera.

Back in Paris, the adventure started afresh. Moreover, it seems that the poet thought of marrying Dridri.[7] Even if the affair had not gone this far, Alecsandri's father had sufficiently serious reasons to be displeased with his son's behavior. He had come to see him in Paris during the summer of 1849 and had certainly heard about this liaison from his friends. The old man loved and appreciated his offspring and had always given in to him, but in this matter he found it difficult to approve. We do not know if they discussed it, but it is certain that once back in Moldavia his father exerted all sorts of pressure on him to make him abandon Paris. Eventually he sent him an ultimatum threatening to cut off the funds that, of course, came exclusively from the family, if he did not come to terms within a month.

This was the decisive argument that persuaded the poet; he finally left Paris on December 19, 1849. From a political point of view, his return to Jassy offered no problem, for Sturdza had been replaced by Grigore Ghica, an enlightened man, fond of culture, who had given a general pardon to all fugitives of 1848 and who knew Alecsandri very well. On the other hand, the role of the émigrés no longer seemed necessary; nor, in view of their dissensions, was it any longer possible for them to keep it up. Alecsandri's first political activity had not left him many illusions, nor had it inspired him with enthusiasm for action in general, but he did not give up hope for the future.[8] He realized that his modified objective required different methods, and he thought up a new activity that pursued the same purpose but that employed something less ephemeral than the press: Alecsandri invented literary propaganda.

This propaganda is merely another aspect of the engaged literature we have seen practiced by Alecsandri in his plays. In them, he drew attention to social shortcomings; through the press in Paris he had endeavored to illustrate the political problems of his nation. This time he proposed to reveal to the Rumanian reading public the existence of a collective Rumanian soul. Its presence seemed to him sufficiently proved by the popular poetry which he had busily collected during the preceding years and which he now decided to bring out. The manuscripts of the copies forming this collection had been brought to him in Paris by his father, and he started sending them off for publication to the review *Bucovina*, the editors of which were the Hurmuzachi brothers. The first appeared with an introductory study about "The Rumanians and Their Poetry," an ambitious attempt at synthesis in which pure literary interest is outstripped by historical and patriotic vision.

Immediately after his return to Jassy, his father, who had just been appointed director of the State Archives, arranged to pass this post on to him on February 3, 1850, meaning to give him a basis for financial independence. But Alecsandri's life continued to center on literature. In the years that followed he devoted himself mostly to the theater, either because he knew it well from his association with Dridri or because the theater, as he says himself, was the only means left to him (since the press was strictly supervised) of addressing the Rumanian public. But the theater itself was no freer than the press, and the plays written at this time only touch remotely on the great national problems that had preoccupied him in Paris. One clearly sees that the poet does not feel free and is longing for the freedom he enjoyed abroad. His Muse has become modest and remains content with castigating a few absurdities of the rising bourgeoisie—*Cucoana Chirița în Iași* (Madam Chirița at Jassy), April 9, 1850; *Kir Zuliaridi*, 1852; *Cucoana Chirița în provincie* (Madam Chirița in the Provinces), May 8, 1852—; with representing more or less satirically a few typical individuals of contemporary Jassy society—*Soldan Viteazul* (Șoldan the Brave), December 30, 1850; *Mama Anghelușa* (Mother Anghelușa), 1850; *Herșcu Boccegiul* (Herșcu the Pedlar), May 31, 1851—; with the clever localization of a few intrigues borrowed from French boulevard theater—*Scara Mîței* (The Cat's Ladder), April 2, 1850; *Doi morți vii* (Two Dead Men Alive), October 28, 1851—or with reviving the operetta atmosphere in which his peasants live and move, *Crai nou* (New Moon), 1852. There is a great gulf between the debatable merits of these unpretentious comedies and the stir created by the folk poems. In September, 1850, after the review *Bucovina* had ceased to appear, he collected some of them in a volume published in Jassy in 1852, which was followed by a second volume in 1853.

Meanwhile, his only trip abroad was to Cernăuți in November, 1850 in order to accompany his brother Iancu on his departure for Paris, where he then definitely settled.[9] At that time Maria Cantacuzino, one of the most remarkable women of the time, a friend of the poet and of Bălcescu, was also going to Paris, where she too made her home.[10]

Like Rousseau, with whom we already have found some resemblance, Alecsandri had a mania for travel, explicable by his need of sun and warmth and of frequent change of scene. Between May 7 and November 29, 1851, he took a new journey to the West, traveling in Germany and England, and visiting especially Paris. He may still have been thinking of Dridri; but the actress died not long before his arrival in Paris.

In that city he resumed the ties he had formed in the preceding years with the Wallachian refugees, who had not yet been authorized to return to their country, and also with his French friends, including Vaillant, Bataillard, Élias Regnault, and Ubicini. The real reason for this journey is not known. However, in view of some of the publications of the following years, it may be deduced that the poet wished to contact the persons who became his close collaborators and his translators—particularly Ion Voinescu and Ubicini. He returned on the steamer *Széchenyi* which was to take him from Vienna to Galatz, but at the end of November, 1851 near Călăraşi he suffered the shipwreck which he later so humorously described in a prose sketch, *Inecarea vaporului Seceni pe Dunărea* (The Sinking of the Steamer Széchenyi on the Danube).

Out of the literary discussions in Paris emerged the decision to publish on his return a new literary review, of which the Rumanian public of the principalities was sorely in need. In conformity with the idea already expressed—of a literature on a national scale regardless of provisional political frontiers—the review was intended to cement future political union and bore the symbolical title of *România literară* at a time when Rumania did not yet exist. The first number was issued in the spring of 1852. The publication had been authorized by the Moldavian government, but the review was confiscated before distribution and was then suppressed. The reasons for this change of attitude are not properly known. The most decisive may have been the presence of Nicolae Bălcescu and of Dimitrie Bolintineanu among the collaborators; both had been exiled from Wallachia for having taken a part in the revolution of 1848, and their collaboration might have raised difficulties with the Wallachian government and, beyond it, with the Petersburg "protectors."

In September, 1852, Alecsandri began again on a journey abroad, which was to last almost two years. His departure at that time and through Galatz does not seem to have been due to pure chance. In Galatz he had a short and dramatic meeting with Nicolae Bălcescu. After years of illness, leading in the West a painful life full of privations, personal worries, and above all of patriotic preoccupations that very deeply affected him, Bălcescu was now a dying man whose only wish was to return to his own country to die. That was the reason of his coming to Galatz; but the reactionary government of Prince Ştirbey had not allowed him to cross the frontier.

Documentation about those tragic moments is scarce. It appears that Bălcescu's last hope was to obtain at least the right to die in Moldavia, but the Moldavian authorities did not permit him to disembark from the ship on which he had sailed from Constantinople. Alecsandri saw him then for the last time either because the meeting had been prearranged or because his arrival in Galatz accidentally coincided with that of his friend. He could do nothing to make Bălcescu's last days easier, and they parted, never to see each other again. Bălcescu was obliged to return through Constantinople to Italy, and he died in Palermo on November 29 of the same year.

From Galatz, Alecsandri continued his journey on the Danube to Vienna and thence on to Paris where he arrived in October. In spring of 1852 his brother had married in Paris Noémie Guillard, a Parisian related to Ferdinand de Lesseps. Probably to make the acquaintance of his new family, both the father and the sister of the poet came to Paris in February, 1852 for a stay of about two months. The poet was then receiving from the printer the volumes which he had come to prepare: his first collection of original verse, *Doine și lăcrămioare* (Doinas and Lilies of the Valley), (1853), in a most elegant edition, such as he probably could not have obtained in Jassy;[11] *Les Doinas, poésies Moldaves* (The Doinas, Moldavian Poems) (1853), translated into French by Ion Voinescu; and volume II of *Poezii populare,* printed in Jassy but with texts sent from Paris. He himself supervised the printing in Paris of Ion Ghica's *Dernière occupation des Principautés danubiennes* (Last Occupation of the Danubian Principalities) (1853).

After these publications were finished and his father had left Paris, Alecsandri went to the spa of Biarritz in August or September. There he met an Englishman, Benedict John Angell,[12] with whom he decided to travel in Spain: it was an old dream of his, born of his love of sun and local color, of Victor Hugo's *Orientales,* and perhaps not less of Kogălniceanu's reminiscences. Though dreamed of and discussed at length, the journey was particularly capricious and full of improvisations and a juvenile fantasy that makes all the charm of the account of the trip later published by the poet.

From Biarritz a trip to Spain should be neither long nor difficult, but the two comrades managed to avoid the shortest way and arrived at Madrid by way of Marseilles and Tetuan. They traveled from Biarritz through Toulouse and Marseilles, where they embarked on a merchant ship to Gibraltar, arriving on September 27. Between October 1 and 9, they undertook an excursion into the continent of Africa and then returned to Gibraltar whence, through

Cadiz, Alecsandri went on to Seville. He visited Córdoba, Granada, and Aranjuez and arrived in Madrid on November 7. He remained in the capital of Spain until December 9, perhaps in the house of, or in any case in close connection with, the marquis of Bedmar, who was married to a Moldavian whom Alecsandri must have known, Lucia Palady, the future inspiration of the Spanish writer Juan Valera.[13] Later, in the coach on the way back to France, he met Prosper Mérimée with whom he kept in touch and whose works he came to know well and to consider a model worthy but difficult to imitate.[14]

The Spanish episode was a ray of light in Alecsandri's life that was also to permeate his work. His account of the first part of the tour—including the travel through the south of France, the voyage to Gibraltar and the African journey through Tangiers and Tetuan—reflects a deep interest in picturesque novelty. It is regrettable that he did not likewise describe the second part of his journey; he has nonetheless put into verse some of his impressions of Andalusia and the romantic vision of Moorish Granada. Alecsandri's Spain is the one he had found earlier in Victor Hugo, Mérimée, and Washington Irving.

Back in Paris, Alecsandri undertook in June–July, 1853, a journey to London, the object of which we do not know. In Paris in the autumn of the following year, news reached him that his father had died on August 3, 1854. This news decided Alecsandri to return to Moldavia. His return marks the end of the idle waywardness of his youth, protected from material worries by the knowledge that a letter home would settle them. Family life was likewise at an end, for none of his near relatives were left to him: both parents were dead, Iancu lived in Paris, and Catinca had long since made a home for herself.[15] For a man so fond of people, light, and warmth, life was becoming a void.

As for his material situation, his father had bequeathed him a fair enough fortune: two houses in Jassy, the estate of Mirceşti, and others at Borzeşti and Pătrăşcani in the district of Bacău. The poet, incurable optimist as he was, no sooner become sole master than, recalling his childish games with the little Gypsies at Mirceşti, he made haste to assemble all his Gypsy slaves in order to tell them that from that moment on they were all free men. "A splendid day!" Alecsandri was to exclaim later when he remembered that disinterested gesture. But he did not fail to note that after six months the same slaves had come to him weeping and besought him on their knees to take them back as slaves as in the good old days.[16]

What must be stressed is the consistency of Alecsandri's ideas. This characterizes his conduct all through the following years which were to bring the much-desired union and the consolidation of the national state. From the point of view of the poet's life, we may distinguish during this period three different phases: the preparation for, achievement of, and international recognition of the union.

Exactly as the revolutionaries of 1848 had foreseen, national unity, having been opposed by the Great Powers, could only emerge as the result of a conflict between these powers. The occasion was at last offered by the Crimean War. The year 1855 was a moment of active and feverish expectation. Owing to the new situation, the poet could at last publish the review he had already planned in 1852, *România literară*. Faultlessly presented and of high literary quality, it ran from January 1 to December 3, 1855. It was suppressed by the government's orders when, in greeting with enthusiasm the princely decree abolishing slavery, the editors, probably through the pen of Ion Ionescu, implied that the emancipation of the peasants would soon unavoidably follow.

But, as usual, the poet could not long remain inactive. Although now director of a review that required his presence and certainly held his interest, although appointed on December 15, 1854 for a term of ten years director of the National Theater in Jassy, his wanderlust was stronger than any tie. In July, 1855, he again started for Paris on the pretext of visiting the Universal Exhibition, and he returned in October by way of Constantinople. On the boat he accidentally met his old friend Ion Ghica, who was Bey of Samos at the time. In the capital of Turkey he visited his Paris friend, the journalist Baligot de Beyne, and with him planned a visit to the Crimean battlefields. They spent a week on the front, from November 27 to December 5, visiting the redoubts around Sevastopol on the grounds of gathering information.

At the Congress of Paris convened in March, 1856, the two principalities obtained the abolition of the Organic Regulation, which was the basis of their political organization, and of the Russian protectorate. Elections were to be organized in Wallachia and Moldavia under the control of an international commission for settling the future organization of the principalities. This started a tough fight to obtain a majority for, or against, the union in the future assemblies (Divans ad hoc).

The role of Alecsandri in the struggle for the preparation of the union was to be a most important one. He was responsible for the *Hora unirii* (The Union Hora) (1857) soon to become popular; the propagandist sketch *Păcală și Tîndală* (Păcală and Tîndală) (1857) in which one of the characters convinces the other of the necessity and advantages presented by the union; *Cinel-cinel* (Riddle-me-ree) (1857), a comedy glorifying peasant life, in which incidental allusion is made to the artificiality of the frontier between the two countries; and *Cetatea Neamțului* (The Citadel of Neamț) (1857), which glorifies the national past. At the same time, he actively fought against the *locum tenens* sent by the Turks to govern provisionally during the elections. Disorderly incidents occurred, and complaints against the lieutenant were brought before the commission; on this occasion Alecsandri was one of the delegation that went to Bucharest to report to the commission. In August, 1857, Alecsandri went to Paris again, this time for a year for reasons of health. He had taken an active part in preparing for the elections, and he had himself been elected deputy, so that his presence was required. Yet excessive excitement was not for him, and as he himself told his new friend Édouard Grenier, he did not have the makings of a minister.[17]

Yet, hardly back from his Parisian escapade, he was nominated minister of foreign affairs in the Moldavian cabinet, on October 25, 1858. The first measure he took in this capacity was to ensure the liberty of the press, hitherto unknown in Moldavia. Already a deputy of the assembly that was to elect the future prince of Moldavia, Alecsandri was at the same time one of the thirty-eight possible candidates. But as the Unionist party could not agree on a single candidate and was endangering its situation in face of an opposition that was in a minority but had only one candidate, Alecsandri solemnly refused the chance offered to him during a meeting of the majority on January 15, 1859. This gesture opened the gates to unionist victory, for it allowed the votes to concentrate on the person of Alexandru Cuza, elected prince of Moldavia on January 17. On February 5, the elective assembly of Wallachia chose the same prince who was not even a candidate there. This last minute improvisation obtained a personal and nominal union of the two principalities, a union which neither fulfilled nor contradicted the provisions of the Paris Convention.

Of the three phases of the union, the first two were thus accomplished. It remained to obtain recognition of the *fait accompli* by the signatory powers of the Paris Convention who had guaranteed the maintenance of peace in the Danube basin. In order to make them swallow the pill, Cuza decided to explain directly to the six interested governments the vital importance of the union for the two principalities and for European peace. With this aim, he sent, as unofficial representatives, Alecsandri to Paris, London, and Turin; Costache Negri to Constantinople; and Ludovic Steege to Vienna and Berlin. This first diplomatic mission entrusted to the poet, from February to May, 1859, was far from easy because of the conflicting interests of the Great Powers and because the envoy represented an unrecognized government.

Alecsandri began with Paris, where difficulties were less than in London, partly because Napoleon III was naturally tempted to counteract Austria's intentions, and also because this ex-*carbonaro* was inclined to listen with more good will to the claims of a small nation that dared talk of independence and liberty. And indeed the reception he met with in Paris was particularly encouraging. He was received in audience by Count Walewski, the foreign minister, and then by the emperor, whom he saw three times—on his arrival, on his return from London, and on his return from Turin. It was again the French government that smoothed the envoy's way to London—where he encountered more obstacles because of British consideration toward the Turks—and then to Italy. In Turin his reception could not but be good, for Italy's political problems were at that time very similar to those of the united principalities and because Austria was the principal obstacle to the fulfillment of their common aspirations.

At the beginning of April, Alecsandri's mission was accomplished. The results were excellent. France's patronage and that of the emperor himself were ensured as was also Britain's benevolent neutrality. The union was not an immediate fact, but the way was definitely cleared—the more so, as Austria's opposition was to be annulled almost at the same time by the campaign launched in Italy. Alecsandri took advantage of this journey to observe the new war. Italy was fighting for her territorial integrity against the same outdated Habsburg imperialism that, sooner or later, national Rumanian feeling would have to confront. His strictly diplomatic mission once accomplished, Alecsandri visited Italy again, especially the battle fronts, from April to June, being present at the battles of Palestro and Magenta.

Returning to his country after a tour through Rome, Naples, and Pompeii and a new sentimental journey to Constantinople, he arrived in Jassy some time in July, 1859. A few months later he was nominated foreign minister in the Wallachian cabinet formed by Ion Ghica on March, 1860, so that the foreign ministries of the two countries were united in his person. But the governments of Moldavia and Wallachia fell one after another, on April 30 and May 28, 1860, respectively, to the great satisfaction of the foreign minister. It was to Mircești that he hastened as soon as he was free, to enjoy at last "the limitless happiness of watching the triumphal march of a flock of geese."[18]

CHAPTER 3

The Poet's Return to his Tools

MIRCEŞTI was an estate of about two thousand acres, embracing the village of that name, along the railway that leads from Roman to Paşcani. The railway did not exist in 1860; it was inaugurated six years later. Alecsandri's isolation consequently was complete. Politics had not been his free choice but an obligation; he withdrew as soon as he found that his presence could be dispensed with.

It was no secret to his friends that the poet was not living alone at Mircesti. As early as 1856 he had had in Jassy a liaison with Paulina Lukasiewicz, a very young girl and, it is said, a very beautiful one.[1] She came from a humble family and was what in Paris one would call a *midinette*. The liaison had lasted some months in the midst of a whirl of amusements that seemed to be a feature of Jassy social life during those years of tiresome waiting. In the summer of 1857 Alecsandri had left as usual for Paris. On his return, he learned that Paulina had given birth to a girl, on November 15, 1857. The comedy had turned to drama, and dramas horrified Alecsandri.

The solution was not easy to find. For a man of honor, as honor was conceived in high society at that time, there should have been no problem, for such things had happened before and were solved by a small allowance for the child. There was no other formula possible, as the difference of class was too great. But it is evident that Alecsandri had other ideas about honor and that scruples of caste could not ease his conscience. His first thought seems to have been to marry and legalize a bond that he had broken by his departure to Paris, but which had not left him indifferent.[2] The marriage, however, affected the whole society with which he was connected. The man who was to be a candidate for the throne of Moldavia at the beginning of 1859 could not in 1858 have given a legal status to his clandestine connection with Paulina. The projected marriage was postponed. Nonetheless, Alecsandri took care of the material situation of both mother and child, ensuring a home

43

for the former and making her in time the actual mistress of his house of Mirceşti where she was already installed in 1860.

The poet thus had a family again. Paulina was a humble woman, almost illiterate, but she surrounded Alecsandri with the affection and warmth he constantly needed and chased away the solitude that he hated. The place he gave Paulina called for no sacrifice on his part but brought him comfort, and at the same time he did not betray the oath he had taken after Elena's death never to marry.[3]

It might be objected that the solution, though convenient, was not the best either for Paulina or for the child's future or for Elena's memory. But for Alecsandri himself? For the first time in his life, Alecsandri had to deal with a problem. Until then, all had been smooth going—even unhappiness: the death of his beloved had been something he could do nothing about. Now his fate depended upon a choice. For the first time he suffered from complexes, and it is most probable that his need for tranquillity weighed heavily in the balance of his ultimate decision. Almost in a day, Alecsandri became settled and withdrawn, like a snail which, after loitering all summer in the sun, retires to his tiny house when autumn and rainy days have come.

At Mirceşti he lived the life of a squire. But he was an odd squire, one who gazed at his poplars on the meadow not to estimate what sum he ought to ask for the timber but to watch life pulsing in the nests and buds. Even when a storm broke or the harvest was flooded, it was Paulina who reckoned the losses and thought of remedies; the poet only saw the grandeur of nature unchained. And, as foreseen in his life program,[4] he now had all the leisure he needed for executing his many literary projects and also for traveling.

It is during this period that the first of his comedies to be weightier in its structure and in its treatment of social problems, *Lipitorile satelor* (The Village Bloodsuckers), was written: he also wrote the comedy *Sgîrcitul risipitor* (The Spendthrift Miser), *Rusaliile* (The Wicked Fairies) and the monologues *Clevetici* and *Sandu Napoilă* at this time. He undoubtedly began editing a series of prose writings which were finished when he was in Paris in the following year, including the diary of his journey to the Italian front in 1859 and that of his excursion to the Crimea in 1855.

The first occasion for travel arose in the following spring and involved an absence of two years spent, as usual, in Paris. It was not a pleasure trip but a new mission from Cuza to the governments of Paris and Turin in connection with a most complicated diplomatic question.[5] Alecsandri was the obvious person to bring a mission of this kind to a satisfactory end. It is probable that the decision was also made because of an arrangement with his brother Iancu, who was in charge of the Rumanian agency in Paris,[6] and whom he was to replace as long as Iancu needed to be away in order to see to his affairs in Rumania; nor is the idea that still persisted in his mind—of finding a way for settling abroad like his brother— to be totally excluded.

In Paris and Turin he succeeded in clarifying the doubts entertained by the two cabinets, and, as soon as he finished his task, remained content with the modest and probably unpaid post of replacing the official agent of the principalities.

This seems to have been the time when he started to write the comedy that was later to bear the title *Boieri și ciocoi* (Nobles and Upstarts) and which for the moment is called *Ciocoii dinainte de 1848* (Upstarts before 1848). He also drew up *Extract din istoria misiilor mele politice* (History of My Political Missions), which he claimed at the time he would allow to be published only posthumously, but which he published himself in 1878; he arranged and completed his collection of popular poems (printed in 1866) and published in Paris a *Grammaire de la langue Roumaine* (1863) that he had probably begun in Moldavia and signed with the pen name V. Mircesco.

His dreams during this time were, as usual, impossible escapism. The weary poet was trying to recapture his lost youth in fresh landscapes. This idea had become an obsession and the poet seriously prepared for a journey somewhere far away—he considered going to Japan. It was probably in this connection that he had decided in 1861 to sell his estate of Pătrășcani, for to travel as he was accustomed, and so far, was an expensive undertaking even for a man free of immediate material worries. His friends grew alarmed. Costache Negri wrote to chide him for insistently planning the realization of such an expensive and ill-advised whim. Alecsandri was no common tourist, but a man who could render great services to his country. The poet's answer, was extremely lucid, affectionate, logical, wise: there is no question of whim but of a long-cherished dream; he had not planned it alone but with Negri himself; nor had he given up the idea of being useful to the community, although he did not see this usefulness in the shape of a ministerial portfolio.[7]

And, stating that the only difference between himself and his stern friend was that he preferred to be indulgent toward the sins of others, Alecsandri confessed that his own sins were travel and women. The latter was a sin he had paid for. Maybe he persisted in it; almost certainly so, for he spent too much time away from Mircești, and it was not in his character to boast without ground for it—if this is a boast, which is far from sure. But even if he went on impenitently sinning, his past experiences must have taught him at least to conceal this failing, for which we have no other evidence to-day. His letter was sensible; yet he managed to be even more sensible. He neither went to Japan nor sold his estate. He remained content with bathing at Dieppe, after Iancu had returned to Paris, and the following summer took the road back to Mircești.

In September, by way of Vienna and Giurgiu, he returned to Bucharest and reported to the prince on his mission. On this occasion he offered Princess Elena Cuza the popular poems he had published, foresaking his author's rights in favor of the asylum for abandoned children which the princess had founded in the capital. He then left for Mircești, which became his domicile from that time until 1885, when he took charge of the legation in Paris. From time to time he paid short visits to Jassy and Bucharest; he did not, of course, give up his periodic visits to Paris, but his and his family's home was definitely established in Mircești. It was there that all major political events of the following years were to find him. It was from there that he watched the authoritarian government of Kogălniceanu, with whom he no longer sympathized; the demagogic progress of the Liberal party; the abdication of Cuza compelled by a plot on February 11, 1866; the first government formed after the *coup d'état* by none other than his old friend, Ion Ghica; and the arrival in the country on May 10, 1866, of Prince Carol von Hohenzollern.

During all this time the poet occupied himself exclusively with his literary work. He devoted himself to his poems, which he published again in 1863 under the old title of *Doine și lacrămioare,* but with substantial additions comprising his third cycle, entitled *Mărgăritărele* (Lilies of the Valley); to *Poezii populare* (Popular Poems), published in 1866 in a handsome volume considerably augmented in comparison to the edition of 1852–53; and to the stage for which he wrote in 1863–66 most of his monologues and the comedies *Harță răzeșul* (Harță the Yeoman), *Arvinte și Pepelea*

(A. and P.), and *Drumul de fier* (The Railway), with an attempt at drawing-room comedy, *Concina* (The Game of Cards).

At the end of 1866 on his way to Paris, he stopped in Cernăuți, where he was given a grand reception organized by the Hurmuzachi brothers and all his Bucovinan friends. In Paris he visited the Universal Exhibition and immediately went on to Nice in search of warmer sunshine. He returned to Moldavia in July for a short stay; prompted by the example of his brother, whose three daughters were at school in Paris, he set off again with his daughter Maria and left her in a boarding school for young ladies at Neuilly.

The Rumanian Literary Society, founded in 1866, which in 1879 became the Rumanian Academy, counted Alecsandri among its members as early as June 2, 1867. Alecsandri took part in the work of the first session but quickly kept aloof because of the Latinist mania possessing most of its members, an exaggeration he often made fun of in his comedies as well as in his correspondence. He closely collaborated, however, with another literary-academic society that had been founded earlier in Jassy: the famous *Junimea* (Youth), inspired by Iacob Negruzzi (the son of his old friend Costache Negruzzi) who had begun to publish in 1867 the important review *Convorbiri literare* (Literary Conversations).

This independent group, a literary circle rather than a formal society, Alecsandri had joined in September, 1867. From that moment on, Alecsandri was an assiduous contributor to the review with his own verses and articles, and he also helped it by his personal connections and by recommending other authors' articles to the editors. Prompted by his infallible instinct, his good taste, and his long literary experience, he immediately realized that *Junimea* acted as a valuable leaven. Alecsandri, who was no longer of the age of the Junimists, but who nonetheless needed an intelligent public and the warmth of sympathetic appreciation, found contact with them a strong stimulant and the seed of a veritable literary renewal. After the influence of Kogălniceanu at the beginning, and that of Bălcescu in middle age, *Junimea's* atmosphere of youthful emulation was decisive for the literary destiny of Alecsandri.

In spite of all that, Alecsandri is no Junimist. Nor could he have been one, for their literary opinions coincide only tangentially. Alecsandri represented a heroic generation, for whom national problems had the highest priority; this historical factor constrained him to set the national element above everything. On the other hand, the Junimists represented a critical and "esthetic" generation, one that believed in art as an independent finality, almost as in a religion. To them, Alecsandri was respectable but outmoded.

From Alecsandri's point of view, the *Junimea* circle had a beneficent influence upon him, not only as a stimulant, but also as a stabilizer. Until that moment, the author's literary and especially his poetical production had been abundant but capricious and dispersed. As Alecsandri very often found no review to publish his writings, his verses had filled drawers from which they were taken out when some happy occasion arose, while his comedies were played without being printed. Now, since *Convorbiri literare* appeared regularly, there was reason for Alecsandri to regulate his output. From now on, his writing became more organized and systematic, for it answered an immediate purpose; his works also acquired more amplitude and cohesion. At the same time, the existence of an esthetic criticism obliged him to reconsider his principles, with interesting effects upon the new form of his art. Thus, the first years of regular contribution to the review (1868–69) produced the cycle *Pasteluri* (Pastels), which show a manifest unity in their variety and are much superior in quality to his former poems.

In March, 1869, he agreed to stand in the elections and was elected deputy. This contradiction to his new style of life is partly explained by the insistence of Kogălniceanu, minister of the interior at the time, whom, as we know, Alecsandri no longer appreciated with the enthusiasm of his younger days. The poet justified himself on the ground that he accepted out of curiosity, as he wished to study a political assembly, just as a literary experience. But he did not take his political mission seriously, for he went abroad again in 1869.

From Paris, where he spent the winter, he went on to Nice in the spring of 1870; in Cannes he visited Mérimée, who died a few months later. In summer he returned to Paris, probably in order to see his daughter at boarding school. In the company of Paulina he went to Arcachon, where the outbreak of the Franco-German War obliged them to return to Moldavia, while Maria took refuge in London. After the war Alecsandri returned to Paris in the summer of 1872 with Paulina; and so he returned again in the following years until 1876 when he brought Maria home. She was now twenty years old. Her father loved her and liked to have her near him, but her presence in the house entailed a delicate problem—that of her illegitimacy.

With her in mind, Alecsandri decided twenty years late to legalize his connection with Paulina. He married her in the most discreet manner possible at Mircești, on October 3, 1876; the fact that Maria was already in Moldavia seems to prove that the poet had hesitated and postponed that solution until the very last minute, for a year later, on October 21, 1877, Maria married Dimitrie Catargi, the son of one of Elena Negri's cousins.[8] One gathers from Maria's reminiscences that the idea of marriage was still repugnant to Alecsandri because of the abiding memory of Elena and that he made the sacrifice for his daughter's sake.

During these years, until 1878, the poet's life was all method and monotony. He contributed to *Convorbiri literare* and collected his complete works in an impressive series of eight volumes (1875–76) and began the new series of epic poems that he was later to collect in the volume entitled *Legende* (Legends) (1875).

He did not write anything new for the theater but in 1874 published the comedy *Boieri și ciocoi* (Nobles and Parvenus), begun much earlier; it might be said that from the point of view of the drama, this period was one of stagnation. The author seems to have abandoned light comedy and vaudeville sketches and had not yet decided to start on the serious plays that were to be his major preoccupation in the following years.

The year 1877 is the date of the War of Independence. The campaign against Turkey—although the result of a precarious alliance with the tsarist empire—roused great enthusiasm in Rumania, not only because of its objective, but also because, whatever its results, it was the first Rumanian political act at international level after two hundred years of absence from the European stage. Alecsandri felt obliged to make what contribution he could to the war.

He who had visited the battlefields of the Crimea and of Italy now regretted that he could not see those of the Balkans because of his age[9] and, more probably, because of his frail health. Although he disliked delivering lectures, he gave them in various provincial towns to raise funds for the care of the wounded. But his greatest contribution lies in the series of patriotic poems published in *Convorbiri literare* and later in 1878 in a volume entitled *Ostașii noștri*

(Our Soldiers), which is a glorification of the young Rumanian army's heroism.

Toward the end of 1877, when the Balkan war was raging, Alecsandri found time to send a poem, *Cînticul gintei latine* (The Song of the Latin Race), to the competition on this subject announced by the Society for the Study of Romance Languages at Montpellier, the prize consisting of a bronze cup offered by the Catalan poet Alberto Quintana y Combis. The jury, composed of Mistral, Quintana, Baron de Tourtoulon, Doctor Obedenaru, and the Italian philologist Graziadio Ascoli—representing five Romance languages—met at Montpellier on May 19, 1878 and awarded the prize to Alecsandri. On May 22 the cup was solemnly handed over to a representative of the poet in the setting of a great festivity at which over 60,000 people were present. It was a triumph for the Rumanian poet. News of the prize was received in Rumania with an enthusiasm which in retrospect may seem exaggerated. But the Rumanian public felt that it was being freed from a complex, exactly as the former generation had on the first night of *Iorgu de la Sadagura*. For the first time the voice of a Rumanian poet was being heard beneath Western skies, while until then the Rumanian people had always been spectators. Rumanian poetry could not but be proud of this coming of age; it seemed to put the finishing touch to the political and military effort of that year.

Alecsandri could not visit Montpellier personally before April–May, 1882. On this occasion he visited several centers of the meridional literary movement such as those of Avignon and Forcalquier, Béziers, and Albi. Everywhere, his reception was equally festive, displaying the same southern exuberance as did the Bucharest and Jassy festivities. The most significant episode of this triumphant expedition seems to have been the obligatory pilgrimage to Maillane, residence of Mistral, who reigned over Provençal poetry as incontestably as did Alecsandri over Rumanian. The meeting and conversation seem to have made a profound impression on our poet and, if we are to believe him,[10] on the Provençal bard too.

In the years 1879–84, we see the poet making a sustained effort in the direction of historical drama—a field he had not explored and in which one is aware of his difficulty as well as of his tenacious will to overcome it. *Despot Vodă* (Prince Despot), written in 1878–79, was played for the first time in Bucharest on September 30, 1879. His second historical drama, *Fîntîna Blanduziei* (The Fountain of Bandusia), originally entitled *Horaţiu* (Horace), was written in winter 1882–83 and was produced in Bucharest on March 23, 1883. Finally, *Ovidiu* (Ovid), finished on December 3, 1884, was not produced until March 9, 1885. Meanwhile, he also wrote for the theater the popular fairy tale *Sînziana şi Pepelea* (S. and P.) (1881) and the farce *Sfredelul dracului* (The Devil's Gimlet) (1881). The poet would have liked to extract from *Ovidiu* an opera libretto in French for music to be composed by Gounod, but this project did not come into effect, as Alecsandri did not finish the libretto. Similarly he had thought earlier, in 1883, of translating *Sînziana şi Pepelea* as a fairy tale play to be produced in London, but this also came to nothing.[11]

In the meantime, the poet's political activity had been more or less nil. He was elected a senator in 1884 but did not often attend the Senate's sessions. Otherwise he lived in relative retirement from public life, perhaps on account of his ever worsening health. Relations with Prince Carol had at first been formal but became closer after 1877, owing to Alecsandri's patriotic compositions and also to the literary inclinations of Princess Elizabeth, well known as a writer under the name of Carmen Sylva. After 1880, he even became a familiar figure at court and was quite often invited to the castle of Peleş at Sinaia, where he repaid hospitality by occasional verses. Invitations to political action were not lacking. In February, 1878, Kogălniceanu, the foreign minister, wanted to prepare European opinion for the approaching peace, and he let Alecsandri know that he counted upon him for the mission to Rome. The poet refused on the plea that he felt the cold too severely, and the four telegrams sent by the minister, in order to convince him that Rome was no colder than Mirceşti, did not succeed in drawing him out of his den.[12] He was nominated vice-president of the Senate, but, like those commendatory abbots who never set eyes on their monastery, he did not trouble to go to Bucharest.

At last, on January 31, 1885, he was sent as plenipotentiary minister to Paris; we do not know what induced him this time to accept. As the old nostalgia for Paris probably still persisted he may have told himself that it was easier for him to settle on the banks of the Seine than to undertake the same journey every year. The fact is that, settled in Paris, he went on making the same yearly journey, but in the reverse direction. Life in Paris could not restore to him his lost health or his flagging inspiration; we sense how anxiously he watched the latter and lost it, the more he tried to rouse it. In fact, he lived as much in the south of France, where he went in search of sunshine, and in Mircești, where he spent prolonged holidays, as in Paris.

Toward the end of 1887, there appeared the first symptoms of the ailment that was ultimately to destroy him, a cancer of the lungs. His last years were given over to hopeless nursing, but it seems that he himself did not realize his actual state until very late. On June 4, he was back in Mircești. It was his last holiday and the last of his pain. On August 22, 1890, he closed his eyes forever, in his house at Mircești. Close to it, a mausoleum has been built where he rests to this day.[13]

CHAPTER 4

Popular Poems

THE volume *Poesii populare ale Românilor* (Popular Poems of the Rumanians) is the most important and at the same time the least original of all poetical works published by Alecsandri. This is no paradox if we remember what has been said in the preceding chapters of our author's peculiar type of poetical inspiration, his possibilities as a writer, and his conception of the poetic act as conscious creation and as an act of will.

However that may be, if we start our study of Alecsandri's poetry with this popular cycle, it is not because of its importance in the ensemble of his poetical works under consideration but mainly because, from the very beginning, popular poetry was to Alecsandri an example and a kind of schooling without which it would be impossible to understand the evolution of his art. Even chronology indicates the same priority. The volume of *Poesii populare* was issued one year before the first volume of original poems. It is true that the latter had been published in reviews and calendars, so that a superficial glance might give the illusion that his original verses in *Doine* were the poet's first work. This conclusion is only a half-truth. Alecsandri had a knowledge of popular poetry and had been enthusiastic about it before he ever attempted his first poetical compositions in Rumanian. We do not know if he had begun to collect the poems with a view to collective publication; but it is quite certain that, soon after his return from his Paris studies, he discovered popular inspiration and dedicated himself to its study with an interest that meant more than an amateur's curiosity. He himself declared that from that time on he decided to abandon his attempts at versification in the French language in order to follow the paths of popular inspiration; even more, he stated that his first poems, those he considered the best, had at the start been prompted by his contact with popular literature.[1] Consequently, it is obvious that Alecsandri's intellectual biography begins with the interest he felt for popular poetry; this fact is the best justification for giving it priority.

Today, for the most part, we misunderstand Alecsandri's enthusiasm for popular poetry. The interest he shows for popular inspiration must not be mistaken for that of a folklorist as we understand
it today. His notions about folklore, his way of interpreting the
material he has collected and published, and even his way of treating
and using it before publishing it evolved through several distinct
phases. We cannot, of course, push analysis too far, inasmuch as
evidence for his conceptions and intentions are lacking, but it
appears broadly speaking that we may distinguish in his attitude
two different periods: the historico-literary and the politico-cultural.

Alecsandri's sustained interest for productions of the popular
muse was not awakened in him by direct contact, for we have seen
that this contact must have existed from childhood; rather, it was
awakened by the example of other literatures. After the resounding
success of the faked historical poems of Ossian and after the discovery of Northern literatures, the European reading public felt
more and more attracted toward the discovery of an authentic
source of local or national inspiration that may be offered in varying
degrees by any established literature. After the post-classical
phase, when the mission of literature appears to have been a sort
of campaign with the object of bringing the art of poetry to a
uniform level, the new generations discovered that national pecu-
liarities do not deserve the indifference which had been shown them.
Romantic love of well-individualized centers, of a picturesque and
motley past, and of garish local color drew attention to cycles of
compositions of a national character that were often neither more
genuine nor more popular than Ossian's poems.

Thus in 1822 Abel Hugo, the brother of Victor Hugo, had published a series of *Romances historiques traduites de l'espagnol*
which awakened an interest for Iberian traditional poetry, until
then almost unknown. About this same time Fauriel published his
famous collection of folk songs from Greece and Vuk Stefanović
Karaźić, his Serbian collection. It is to be presumed that Alecsandri knew these publications, especially the latter which had
quite a resounding success. Though he did not speak Serbian, he
could consult the French translation published by Élise Voïart
under the title *Chants populaires des Serviens* (1834). Furthermore,
Karaźić entertained a correspondence with some Rumanian writers
of that time, among others Gheorghe Asaki, to whom he had sent
a series of Rumanian popular poems collected by him, probably

in the Banat region. Later the compilation of Xavier Marmier, *Chants populaires du Nord* (1842), and that of Le Roux de Lincy, *Recueil de chants historiques français depuis le XII-e jusqu'au XIII-e siècle* (1841–42) probably came into Alecsandri's hands.

The collectors, and with them the reading public, assessed the interest of these compositions more by their value as documents revealing the national historical past than by any literary or esthetic criteria. At a time when nationalism was in full swing and every European people was searching for its own identity, reflected in the memory of the national past as in a mirror, popular poetry made its appearance, says Mickiewicz, like a sort of ark of the covenant between old and new times. In it, added the great romantic, "the nation deposits the trophies of its heroes, the hope of its thoughts, the flower of its feeling."[2] Like Mickiewicz, Alecsandri saw in popular poetry a sort of archive of the national soul, a collective memory and a dispersed treasure that had to be gathered and made known for the nation to recognize itself.

The Rumanian world too was interested in these testimonies of its national past. In his introduction to *Dacia literară* in 1840, M. Kogălniceanu advised young writers to learn by imitating national elements of literature rather than to let themselves be integrated into foreign literary movements. Kogălniceanu himself was not the first to propose the traditional muse as a model; his ideas in this regard coincide with those expressed a year earlier by Heliade Rădulescu in *Curierul Românesc* (The Rumanian Courier) and also by Gheorghe Bariț in *Foaie pentru minte* (Paper for the Mind).[3] In 1845 Bălcescu set himself the task of gathering poems and tales, and, significantly, he recommended this in a strictly historical publication, *Magazinul istoric pentru Dacia* (Historical Magazine for Dacia). Alexandru Russo was as enthusiastic as Alecsandri for this vast enterprise of research and of unearthing the treasures of folklore, and some of the peregrinations and inquiries were undertaken by the two friends together. Finally, in *O şezătoare la ţară* (A Country Gathering) by Anton Pann (1853), we find many elements of folklore and popular poetry. The collection of *Poezie populară* of Atanasie Marienescu (1859) belongs to the same years. Thus, it is obvious that Alecsandri was not isolated.

It seems certain that the inducement to study popular poetry came to him from Kogălniceanu and the program of *Dacia literară*. We know how Kogălniceanu had made him a Rumanian writer by isolating him in the country, where he was induced to write *Buchetiera de la Florenţa*. And we know, on his own confession that Alecsandri was easily influenced.[4] He needed energetic prompting in order to emerge from the rut of minor French poetry, the only form of literature he had practiced up to that moment. All these circumstances are sufficient to justify the opinion that Alecsandri approached popular literature with the idea that in it he would find a literary schooling and a pattern of poetry that deserved to be imitated. The literary program of Kogălniceanu and the first personal contacts of Alecsandri with this movement for the renovation of literature through tradition and nationalism began in 1840. Alecsandri's first known collection of popular ballads is dated to the year 1842. It is possible that he may have transcribed texts sporadically even earlier; in any case, he dedicated himself to this activity in the following years, so that it may be said that when obliged to go into exile in 1848, his collection was practically finished, although he did not publish any part of it until 1849.

Yet the idea of publishing popular texts may not have come to the poet until very late, if we consider that he was not working as a folklorist but was collecting mostly for his own instruction and literary formation. On the other hand, in his mind the term "popular" was far from having the collective and impersonal meaning we give it today. He was convinced that the poems he published under his name in various reviews and calendars, and which represented personal interpretations and elaborations of circumstances or feelings that more or less coincided with the rustic muse, rightly deserved the qualification of "popular". It can consequently be assumed that his intention—if it had at the beginning a precise and conscious form—was to draw on popular inspiration in order to compose on his own account a series of ballads and lyrical poems, personal in form and traditional in content. This was being done at the time by many European poets whose example he was acquainted with; an example is Uhland, whom he quotes and who drew on Spanish, French, and German traditions in order to write his own collection of *Balladen und Romanzen*.

But when he published his first popular texts in 1849, Alecsandri's conception had greatly evolved. In the Bucovina where he spent the summer of 1848, in the company of the Hurmuzachi brothers and of a number of intellectuals who often discussed the nation's future and their progressive ideals, popular poetry appeared to him as a political instrument to be used for training minds and shaping opinions. This center, composed of Rumanians who were without a country but who were as responsive as he was to the beauties of *Miorița* (Ewe-Lamb), could not but draw his notice to a community of spirit in which folklore was a link and, as Mickiewicz put it, an "ark of the covenant." The popular poems were no longer a workshop for apprentices in the art of poetry, as they had seemed to him until then, but a school for the nation.[5] This new vision explains the interest, not felt before, with which during the following years he pursued the project of publishing this collection in a volume.

Historical circumstances show him to be right. In the following years, when Rumanian problems were no longer local ones as in 1848, but European, Alecsandri's horizons were further enlarged. As in 1849 the object of the publication had been to keep alive the strength and consciousness of national unity, so in 1855 the problem was to make the Rumanians, who were now soliciting the support of European opinion, known and loved, and by translations published during these years, this target was partly attained.[6] By this means, Alecsandri sought for all Rumanians what Chateaubriand had desired for himself: *de la gloire pour se faire aimer.*

The publication of the popular poems was no easy undertaking, partly because of Alecsandri's many pursuits throughout the years—of wanderings and of political and literary activity—and partly because publications that might welcome such productions were not available. As early as September, 1849, he was able to offer the Rumanian public a series of popular ballads accompanied by two introductory studies in the review *Bucovina*. The first study is an eulogy of popular traditions; the second (February 18, 1850) analyzes three compositions considered by the author as characteristic: *Mihu copilul* (The Lad Mihu), *Păunașul codrilor* (The Forest Peacock), and the famous *Miorița* (Ewe-Lamb). When the Bucovinan review ceased to appear, he published such isolated ballads in *Zimbrul* (The Bison), a Jassy newspaper, and in *Calendarul pe anul 1851* (Calendar for 1851).

In 1852, Alecsandri at last published in Jassy the first brochure of *Poesii populare*. This general title appeared over the actual title of the collection, *Balade (Cîntece bătrînești) adunate și îndreptate de B. Alecsandri* (Ballads—Songs of Our Forefathers—Collected and Corrected by B. Alecsandri). The second series was issued next year, also in Jassy. In 1866 the final collection of *Poesii populare ale Românilor* was published in Bucharest in a beautifully presented

volume containing many additions to the texts that had been published until that date; these were also some editorial variants that
are particularly significant.[7]

Taking into consideration the divisions indicated by the collector, the popular poems are of three kinds: ballads or ancestral
songs; *doine,* or lyrical songs; and *hore,* or songs set to dance music.
The two last sections are by all standards the finest and purest part
of this inspiration. From a strictly folklorist point of view they do
not seem to present such difficult problems to the literary investigator as does the collection of ballads.

In their turn, the latter may be divided into various other series.
Rhetorical manuals of last century divided them more or less as
follows:

(a) Historical ballads, so called because they mention the name
of a prince, such as Negru Vodă, Ştefan cel Mare, or Constantin
Brîncoveanu. But the actual historical character of these compositions is debatable enough and often nonexistent. If such a
historical name does happen to appear, its presence is sometimes
quite accidental and has no immediate connection with the known
past or the person mentioned. On the other hand, the texts where
such names appear do not always present sufficient guarantees of
authenticity. They are sometimes mere personal compositions of
Alecsandri's; in other cases, the name seems to have been added.

(b) Outlaw songs, in which the hero is an outlaw: *Corbea,
Jianu, Bujor, Tunsul, Vidra, Păunaşul codrilor,* and *Mihu copilul.*
These compositions, the most numerous, are founded on a substratum of reality; but the strictly biographical and historical circumstances look the more dim or fantastic as they are more distant
in time.

(c) Domestic ballads, in which conflicts and anonymous actions
are described and in which the heroes of the narrative are more
characters than persons: *Inelul şi năframa* (The Ring and the
Kerchief), *Bogatul şi săracul* (The Rich Man and the Poor), and
Socrul (The Father-in-law).

(d) Supernatural ballads: *Mioriţa* (Ewe-Lamb), *Cucul şi turturica*
(The Cuckoo and the Dove), *Soarele şi luna* (The Sun and the Moon),
Ciuma (Plague), and *Holera* (Cholera), in which we usually recognize
personages of popular mythology and fairy tales in general.

This classification is far from complete, and many of the poems
in the collection do not fit into any of the indicated categories.

Poems like *Toma Alimoş* or *Mogoş Vornicul* might be considered historical if we knew to whom or what period they refer, but the names could as well be conventional and the action be wholly invented. In any case, the majority of these popular ballads have for heroes a series of personages that are neither anonymous nor historical and can only be fitted into categories of this sort by force. It is thus preferable to consider this subdivision as a fairly elastic one. Altogether, we may admit two widely comprehensive categories: the ballads we have termed historical even when not so, and the mythical ballads, which translate into verse the miraculous atmosphere of the fairy tale or put into action a circumstance that might easily happen in reality but that has legendary implications.

We do not intend here to analyze these productions, which do not represent Alecsandri's own poetical art. It is, however, apposite to note—for this involves the author—that, in the light of all that has already been said, the publication of these *Poesii populare* presents two kinds of problems to which the biographer of Alecsandri cannot remain indifferent; namely, their authenticity and their purpose.

Considered in its totality, there can be no doubt that this collection is composed of genuine texts. The majority are known from other collections as well, subsequent to that of Alecsandri, but coming from other regions than those he himself mined. Furthermore, in many cases notes added by the author at the end of the volume indicate the place of collection and sometimes even the name of the person questioned. Finally, Alecsandri has himself told more than once how he rambled through villages and mountains, entering inns, spending nights in sheepfolds, mixing with the crowd at fairs, in search of such texts, the popular character of which, consequently, needs no other certificates.

But the aspect of the whole cannot deceive the investigator as to the heterogeneous character of the material contained in this volume; nor did Alecsandri mean to deceive him. The poet did not make any distinction between collected poems and those made by himself. From his point of view, "popular" was both what came from the people and also what was intended for the people: the best proof of this is that the ideal inspired in him by Elena Negri was all along to become "the popular poet" of Rumanians everywhere. This may explain the fact that in the 1866 volume, among ballads, *doine,* and *hore* collected from the people, he included, with what seems to us surprising casualness, the famous *Hora unirii* written by himself and admitted to this collection because in the meantime it had become "popular." In the same way, when Bălcescu asked if he knew of any popular poem about Mihai Viteazul, whose history he was engaged in writing, Alecsandri answered that he would look out for one, and if he did not find any, he would compose one himself and send it to him.[8] It is to this strange collaboration with folklore that we owe *Cînticul lui Mihai Viteazul* (The Song of Michael the Brave), which was likewise inserted in the collection of *Poesii populare,* and which is popular neither in the sense we give the term today nor in that of a wide diffusion and acceptance by the people.

Faced with these examples, we doubt the authenticity of the whole. If Alecsandri has twice proceeded in this way, how many times has he done so without mentioning it? A superficial glance is enough to convince the reader, even the least expert, that *Hora dela Mircești* (The Mircești Hora), *Dragoș,* and *Visul lui Tudor Vladimirescu* (Tudor Vladimirescu's Dream), have nothing in common with popular poetry—except the wish of a contemporary author to imitate the manner of traditional poetical art. They are undoubtedly the work of Alecsandri. It is appropriate to determine more closely which are the truly popular productions, which are the criteria that guided the poet in his work as collector, and which are the results of his personal intervention.

The determination of popular authenticity is not easy, for Alecsandri has assimilated the possibilities and mannerisms of the popular muse with a mimicry that may deceive the most vigilant attention.[9] The purely formal criteria are not satisfactory, and the strictly documentary ones are sporadic and do not answer all questions. A comparative criterion might be taken into consideration. It seems quite obvious that a poem which does not figure anywhere else except in the collection of Alecsandri and has not been heard of by any other Rumanian folklorist is very likely to be a personal creation of Alecsandri. There are about a dozen such poems: those mentioned above, *Năluca* (The Ghost), *Șoimul și floarea fragului* (The Falcon and the Strawberry Flower), *Magdu, Călătorul* (The Traveler), *Românii depe malurile Dunării* (The Rumanians on the Danube Shores), *Muierușca din Brașeu* (The Lass from Brașeu), *Sîrb-Sărac.*

Yet the problem is not so simple. Among the ballads that we

know of only through Alecsandri is *Păunaşul codrilor,* the first one published by him (1850), and *Român Grue Grozovanul.* The author has noted in both cases the name of those from whom he heard them. It seems therefore that, although they are not met with in any other folklore collection, these ballads must be popular. At the same time, others are just the opposite. *Erculean,* for instance, has been preserved in twenty-five variants, collected in widely different regions, from Banat to Dobruja, and yet it is not in the least likely that it is folklore.[10] Thus, in our present state of knowledge, the problem remains insoluble. We must add that the problem is exclusively ours and did not exist for Alecsandri. For him the fact that authentic popular material coexisted in his collection with his personal contributions was of no importance whatever. Scruples of fidelity and mechanical reproduction never worried him; it may even be said that they concerned him less and less as time went by. The 1852 brochure says as much in its title: the poems have been collected and corrected by Alecsandri; in 1866, they were "collected and arranged," a variant that clearly enough expresses his attitude toward texts transmitted by tradition.

Alecsandri was, in fact, not a folklorist but a poet. Though he knew that in his capacity as collector, he had some obligation of fidelity to truth, his fidelity was not that of a scribe but of a poetical interpreter. It is true that he sometimes happened to hesitate between two variants heard by him and quoted both versions one after another. But he was not prompted by philological scruples; both forms pleased him artistically. His duty as he understood it was to bring forward, not a certain poem, but popular genius; not an image or an episode, but a manner of conceiving life and art. If it is true that he once dreamed of being a great poet, we must not forget that, according to his point of view, great poets "are only the master revealers of the people's poetry."[11]

In reality, Alecsandri was no editor of texts but a popular poet; in a sense, he was a spontaneous collaborator. His procedure had nothing to do with the usual technique of folklore inquiry: it was identical with that of his fiddler or, if this comparison seems out of place, with that of the collective memory which in transmitting assimilates. He listened and learned, but his mind both forgot and filled out. His intervention was yet another link in the endless chain of oral transmission. In contrast with the anonymous poets preceding him, he attached a known name to these anonymous productions, and he fixed the tradition in writing, insofar as a still living tradition allows itself to be fixed.

This explains the fact that Alecsandri assumed the right to mingle his personal inspirations with those of the popular muse. He conceived popular poetry as Lope de Vega, Gongora, and all the poets of the Spanish Golden Century considered the *Romancero*—as common property. Alecsandri has been harshly criticized for the freedom with which he undertook the reproduction of popular texts.[12] This criticism is at once just and unjust. It is just inasmuch as it cannot be denied that Alecsandri was not what we would term today a good collector. But it is unjust, for in this way Alecsandri finds himself accused of not having done the very thing which it was not his wish to do. He had understood that his duty as poet was to cause a poetical shock, an impact on opinion; in order to do so, he used poetical means, as one would expect.

Regarding the authenticity of the texts, his intervention is evident not only in that he added a few compositions of his own but also in that he restored and presented in a correct and coherent way some poems that he himself said he had collected in a disarranged form—incomplete or contaminated—and it is very well known that gaps and corrupt versions are frequent in popular tradition. In his collection, all of the poems are perfectly structured on the basis of genuine material, but with a care for the architectural whole that is generally lacking in strictly folkloric collections. For the most part, these remodelings and transformations, which he called "arrangements", are obviously stylistic improvements, such as the insertion of a few transitional verses where they seem to be lacking, or of more appropriate expressions, simplifications, or amplifications, that always have their artistic logic but are never the result of new research in the field.[13]

As to the second kind of problem presented by *Poesii populare*—the collector's purpose—signs of it are visible in the text itself, but in most cases not clearly enough, so that they have to be sought in the introductory commentaries or in the notes. We already know that the principal purpose of the author was to illustrate the national past by a knowledge of popular epic, considered by the romantics as the remnants of a primitive epos. Alecsandri believed that in most cases this objective had been attained by the mere production of the texts. Here, the notes are content to draw attention to details of history, civilization, or folklore that are, of course, interpreted in the light of the poet's conceptions and personal interest, which also means the national interest of his time. Occasionally, this preoccupation shows itself in a conscious alteration of the text; instead of the text illustrating his historical conceptions, the latter confer a bogus authenticity on what is pure invention.

The true conceptions of Alecsandri—what we might call his folkloristic vision of the Rumanian universe—should be looked for in the apparatus that accompanies the popular texts. The peasant world of the poet, like the national past, was clad in the idyllic colors that characterize his original verses and his rustic comedies. His understanding of the rustic world as a subject for literature was based on the classical and post-classical pastoral; and, from the point of view of appreciating historical atmosphere and the mysterious or legendary past, it was based on the literature of chivalry, especially on Ariosto and Tasso. To look for realism in Alecsandri would be a waste of time.

It was natural for him so to interpret folklore themes as to make his readers see in popular poetry what he himself thought he saw. If we are to believe the commentary which serves as preface to the collection, the hero of the ballad *Mihu copilul* is "a troubadour knight of the middle ages," and the song that petrifies the robbers of the rival band is a scene straight from Ossian, which Alecsandri of course considered to be genuinely medieval. Păunaşul Codrilor to his eyes appeared as one of Tasso's heroes, his heart divided between the thirst for love and for glory. Alecsandri had only to come across the term *zale,* "coat of mail" *(Mihu copilul)*—and we should not be surprised if he introduced the word himself—or *fraţi de cruce,* "brotherhood" *(Balaurul)* (The Dragon), and he maintained that the texts in question dated back to the Crusades. In this way literature imposes itself on history, and folklore will only prove what the collector wants it to prove. As these ballads are more and more elaborated, they recede more and more from folklore.

But Alecsandri's ambitions led him even further. Popular poetry—this image of the people, at once a document of identity and a title of nobility—must reach further back in time and provide evidence for the Latin origin of the race. The poet was brought up in the generous romantic illusion according to which popular literature perpetuates the primitive phase of history. It was a matter of course that in his turn he should seek for traces of Rome in his ballads and, even more, that he should find them before looking for them, inasmuch as he was certain of the result. And that is what happened. Alecsandri did not hesitate to identify Păunaşul Codrilor with the god Pan and connect certain funereal rites with ancient libations and with Charon's obol (*Năluca*); recognize in the wrestling of Moldavian peasants the technique of ancient gladiators *(Păunaşul Codrilor)*; and interpret the word *nevastă,* "wife", as a derivation from *Vesta* with a negative prefix *(Brumărelul)*.

Consequently, it is evident that our way of considering the collection of *Poesii populare* does not concur with the leading ideas of Alecsandri. For us, what makes the publication interesting is the folklore and popular civilization, while to Alecsandri it had begun by being a formative influence and later became the chief factor in an important national process. We approach the book with a kind of objective scruple and regret the freedoms taken by the collector; for him these freedoms were an obligation. Judged from Alecsandri's own point of view, his collection had quite exceptional value. It may be said without any exaggeration that the dozens, perhaps hundreds, of similar subsequent publications taken together do not count for as much as a single one of Alecsandri's arranged ballads. It is not solely a question of chronological merit.[14] The impact he proposed to make was actually made. The people's inspiration, as it emerged from the massive volume of 1866, formed an impressive whole by its proportion, cohesion, variety, clarity, unity of conception, and above all by the new and ineffable quality of the poetry it revealed. However things may evolve, however points of view may differ, if there is such a thing as history of Rumanian literature, *Poesii populare* of 1866 is its first peak, the first that touches the level of universal literature.

It is true that some of the merits mentioned above are those of Alecsandri rather than of the somewhat formless material he had at his disposal. It may be said, for example, that the first masterpiece of Rumanian literature that has never been outmoded, *Miorița,* is timeless and yet dates from 1866. Everyone has understood it thus, and the definitive form, *Miorița* at its best, will always be that of Alecsandri. As Bolintineanu said, Rumanian poetry became Rumanized after 1866. This expression is much more precise than it would at first seem. There had been earlier attempts to nationalize Rumanian culture; and we have mentioned that about 1839–40 all Rumanian intellectuals agreed upon this necessity. Yet in that generation such programs could hope for no real support; while in 1867, when *Junimea* at Jassy was beginning in its review to defend a literature based on esthetic criteria, such a trend could thrive because there was now a literature as a basis: Alecsandri's collection dating from the previous year was a literature in itself. Of course, we do not mean to say that *Junimea* built on the foundation of *Poesii populare*. But the esthetic phase would have remained what Maiorescu himself termed "form without content" if the nationalist phase had not been achieved. Estheticism, which is a reaction, would have had nothing against which to react. The new paths indicated by Alecsandri were followed not only by direct imitators and fellow traditionalists but also by literary currents that developed in opposite directions.

On the other hand, in 1866 Alecsandri's collection had already received European recognition; it had been translated into four languages. The final Rumanian edition had been preceded by the French translation of Ubicini (1855), the English of H. Stanley (1856), the German of W. von Kotzebue (1857), and the Hungarian of Ács Károly (1858).[15] These publications, especially the French one, had had a gratifying reception. To the same period belong a few foreign translations and imitations, testifying that the themes of popular poetry as presented by Alecsandri were of interest and were about to circulate in Europe.[16]

The publishing of the 1866 volume had another and unexpected result. The poems thus circulated to some extent reentered the popular repertory. Some amateur, some literate fiddler would learn the ballads and songs from the printed book instead of having recourse to the living sources of traditional folklore. It thus happens that some later collections, carried out with every guarantee of scientific objectivity, offer variants or versions that can only be explained by Alecsandri's personal intervention. This phenomenon took place almost immediately. The poet himself notes that he happened to hear original verses inserted by him in a certain composition and transferred by some popular reciter to other compositions he himself did not know.[17] What happened to Alecsandri, another popular singer, Anton Pann, wished might happen to himself when he published his verses "from the people gathered and to the people restored." To Alecsandri, this automatic adoption of his modifications was a reason for satisfaction and legitimate pride, as it was the best proof that his undertaking to "arrange" popular poetry had met with success.

CHAPTER 5

Poems

I Doine *(Lyrical Songs)*

ALECSANDRI'S first volume of poems was published in 1853 and represented the harvest of a production spread over a period of ten years. The first Rumanian verses claimed by him that have come to our knowledge were written in 1842—the year in which he first collected ballads. This coincidence is not mere chance.

In 1842, Alecsandri had not the least notion of prosody or of Rumanian poetic art. He certainly could read Rumanian, for he received letters from his parents, and he had probably learned to write the Cyrillic alphabet in his childhood. But this amount of knowledge does not suffice to make a writer. Neither was it easy for him to teach himself, for literary texts might have been numbered on the fingers, and they did not always deserve to be taken as models.

The difficult task of writing started for Alecsandri as soon as he returned to his country from his studies in Paris aged about twenty. His exceptional situation as a young man representative of culture created unavoidable obligations—particularly the obligation to write. In prose he was successful, if not at once, at least at his first known attempt, but at the cost of what subterfuges we shall presently see. It was not so easy with poetry.

Alecsandri had written French verses in Paris, and it was in French that he continued to write when he came back. As the atmosphere in Jassy was fairly cosmopolitan, nobody was astonished that his first published verses (in 1841) were in French.[1] The best proof that he could not have written them in Rumanian is the fact that, because of the bilingual character of the review that published them, they had to be presented in both languages, and the Rumanian translation had to be entrusted to others. This comes out even more clearly in *Buchetiera de la Florenţa* (1840), in which the author had included some verses in French; later, when he had learned to write Rumanian verses, he replaced them by a Rumanian composition.[2]

Hence, in 1840–42, Alecsandri found himself in the odd situation of a poet who does not know how to write verse. This being so, it would be interesting to know what made him begin to write Rumanian verse. As far as we can judge, it must have been a spirit of emulation with friends of his own age and the pressing solicitation of Kogălniceanu on behalf of *Dacia literară*. In order to write Rumanian verse, however, he needed apprenticeship. The collection and study of popular poems gave him his training.

The great merit of Alecsandri as a pioneer poet is that he did not turn to contemporary poetry and established style. He might have learned the art of versifying by following the example of Conachi, Mumuleanu, and other writers of the preceding generation or that of Hrisoverghi and Wallachian contemporaries. In other words, two paths were open to him: that of anacreontic and arcadian lyric, halfway between Gypsy fiddlers' songs and the modern Greek poetry led by Athanasios Christopoulos, a poetry springing from an imitation of Italian Arcady and neoclassical pastoral in general, but reduced to sentimental declamation, langorous and sickly; and that of French preromanticism with its elegiac themes and recently imported rhythms. Neither of these directions was unknown to Alecsandri, and it is evident in his work that he put both to use. His merit, which is a proof of his good taste, is that he subordinated both modalities to a new model—popular poetry. The first of Alecsandri's Rumanian poems were thus stylistic exercises such as any apprentice in poetry might write as his reaction to popular texts and inspiration. Alecsandri never seems to have been a good pupil, but he applied himself so assiduously to the study of popular poetry that he almost immediately succeeded in emulating it; and this intention itself was new in the literature of his time.

All theoreticians of literary reform, Kogălniceanu in particular, considered national literary tradition to be a starting point; for Alecsandri it was a finishing point, that is, an ideal and a model. When others strove to equal Chénier or Lamartine, Ossian or Byron, he dreamed of competing with the popular muse. With the realism that never abandoned him, Kogălniceanu had considered popular literature a source of new energies; for Alecsandri, who always remained an impenitent idealist, the source became an objective.

Like most weaklings who have allowed themselves to be driven along a path, he did not know where to stop. With the mimicry with which he filled out the verses of *Mihu copilul,* he almost mechanically wrote his own *Doină,* and if he had been capable of writing an original *Mihu copilul* of his own, he would have felt himself the happiest and most accomplished of poets.[3] The result of this attitude is that there are very few differences between the collection of *Poesii populare* and the first series of original poems by Alecsandri. The most important is that in his original poems he allowed himself to innovate, adapting metrical schemes that were unknown to the popular poet; but their number is very small. Out of twenty-four poems, three or four are in verses of more than eight syllables, the utmost limit of popular verse.[4] In all other aspects—themes, vocabulary, images, sentiments, and poetical universe—there is almost no dissonance to be found between the two collections. If it does exist, it is not so much owing to his wish for independence as to the difficulty he had of keying his imagination exactly to that of popular mentality.

Direct imitation of popular inspiration was not in the least concealed by the author. On the contrary, two poems of the cycle ostensibly bear the characteristic title of *Doină* (I and XXIII), which is also that of the collection and is peculiar to popular lyric. Two more compositions bear the subtitles "Ancestral Song" (XVII) and "Worldly Song" (XXII), labels which are equally transparent.

The most important composition of this cycle, *Marioara Florioara*, is described as a "legend," like *Erculean,* and apes all the trappings of a ballad; it is true that it is a much later composition, from about 1852, just before the volume was printed. But chronological distance only confirms the poet's wish to maintain himself within the strict limits of popular inspiration in all the verses belonging to this cycle.

He once thought of including *Marioara Florioara* among the ballads published about the same time in *Poesii populare* and thus presenting it as an authentic production of popular imagination.[5] It may be said, in short, that the whole collection of *Doine* depends entirely on popular epic and lyric. With one possible exception *(Baba Cloanța),* there is no need to refer to the two currents predominant in the cultivated poetry of the time in order to explain it.

The *Doine* cycle consists of twenty-four poems written between 1842 and 1853. Eighteen of them were published in *Albina românească* (The Rumanian Bee) of 1843, in the *Calendars* of Kogălniceanu (1843–45), and in the reviews *Propășirea* (1844) and *Bucovina* (1849–50). The others were printed for the first time in the Paris collection in 1853. After that the composition of the cycle suffered no modification whatever.

The title is a manifesto. The *doină* is preeminently a lyrical style;

but the word, as well as the inspiration to which it refers, had no prestige whatever in the circle of poetry readers. The fashion of the time called for meditations and elegies. To give a volume of verse the title *Doine* was a kind of challenge or, if not, a proof of great modesty. Alecsandri was more capable of the second attitude than of the first. He was an unconditional admirer of the genre, and his praise of the *doină* in his prose sketch *O primblare la munți* (A Trip in the Mountains) is famous. There the *doină* personifies Moldavia mourning the loss of her past glory. All the same, the title is inaccurate. The *doină* is a lyrical genre, and half of Alecsandri's compositions included in this cycle are of an epic nature. This confusion of genres is present in all the poet's work; his titles must not be considered as strictly limitative but as simply indicating the tonality of the contents as a whole.

The lyrical compositions are at the level of popular sensibility. *Doină,* the opening poem of the cycle, indicates programmatically the double trend of these inspirations: love songs, which are a rustic equivalent of serenades—*Mîndrulița de la munte* (The Mountain Sweetheart), *Dorul* (Yearning), *Doina iubirii* (The Love Doină), of gallant pastoral in dialogue—*Făt-logofăt* (Prince Charming), *Cinel-Cinel* (Riddle-me-ree), of dancing songs—*Hora* (The Round Dance), and cradle songs—*Dorul Romậncei* (The Rumanian Girl's Yearning): and on the other hand, the outlaw song—*Cîntic haiducesc* (Outlaw's Song), *Strunga,* or patriotic song—*Tătarul* (The Tartar), *Cîntic ostășesc* (Soldier's Song). Halfway between these two sources of inspiration are a series of compositions of a new type, or, rather, a composite one, both epic and lyrical, in which the two previous themes are intertwined: in them all, the loving maiden is an idyllic peasant as before, while the hero is a soldier, an outlaw, or a mysterious stranger—*Sora și hoțul* (The Nun and the Robber), *Crai nou* (New Moon), *Ursiții* (The Destined Husbands), *Strigoiul* (The Vampire), *Ceasul rău* (The Evil Hour), *Sburătorul* (The Incubus).

On the surface, the thematic novelty of this last group consists simply in the association of two already familiar effects. In reality the association does not merely combine the effects but multiplies them and gives them a new intensity. The novel situation, resulting from the obvious difference of level between the two worlds brought into contact—the idyllic with the mysterious—creates tension of a purely romantic character, and the rustic idyl is turned into drama. The romantic tinge comes precisely from the presence of shadow, that is, from the mystery from which the lover temporarily emerges and which in some of the poems suggests a spell *(Crai nou)* or phantoms like the terrifying image of the vampire *(Sburătorul)*.

The relatively large number of poems relying upon this series of effects is symptomatic. What is more, Alecsandri himself probably appreciated the novelty and efficiency of this dramatic device, for he used it repeatedly, broadening the gap between the two protagonists to the ultimate exaggeration of *Baba Cloanţa*. This poem, perhaps the most happily achieved in all the cycle, and in any case the most novel in its structure and dramatic tension, sings of the impossible love of an old witch for a young man who does not materialize and for whom she vainly seeks by incantations, while Satan gloats in the dark.

The structure, the strophic form, the effects of witchcraft, the sinister midnight, and the fantastic cavalcade recall not only folklore but also the ballads of Gottfried August Bürger, and especially the famous *Lenore,* which Alecsandri almost certainly knew through one of the many translations in French of the time. The staging and technical realization are at the same time the most complete and most successful of the whole series. It is consequently strange to observe that it is exceptional in Alecsandri's poetical works, for he never again created such fantasies.

Like *Poesii populare,* the cycle *Doine* includes a series of ballads. Their material is mixed; outlaw songs—*Maghiara* (The Magyar Woman), *Andrii Popa, Groza:* historical ballads—*Altarul mănăstirii Putna* (The Sanctuary of Putna Monastery): fantastic legends—*Marioara Florioara*. The popular categories are exactly repeated. *Altarul mănăstirii Putna* and *Groza* are the only ones to be composed on the metrical patterns of cultivated poetry. The latter has enjoyed a quite exceptional popularity that is probably justified less by its intrinsic merit than by the novelty that made it the first cultivated interpretation of an outlaw theme. The others are mere imitations in a popular key, and it was only by the author's discretion that they were not included in the collection *Poesii populare.*

The ballads are based in varying degrees on fact. *Andrii Popa* is the tale of a real episode, the hero of which had been the poet's uncle on his mother's side, Mihail Cozoni. *Altarul mănăstirii Putna* is the result of a visit paid by the poet to Putna, as *Erculean* had been the result of his visit to the spa of Mehadia; and the same is true of *Maghiara,* eponymous heroine of the river bearing that name. Finally, *Marioara Florioara,* the longest (595 verses of eight syllables), takes up again the facile symbolism of certain themes from *Poesii populare,* which are perhaps no more popular than these; but the poet takes them up again with a gracefulness, a freshness of expression, and a mimetic virtuosity which he never again attained. It is true that in most cases the impression of freshness is due to direct borrowing of popular expressions and even of whole lines from familiar ballads; but the ensemble perfectly recreates the fairy-tale atmosphere. Alecsandri had dreamed of writing a *Mihu copilul* of his own; this ballad suffices to ensure him, if not the glory of a great poet, at least that of a popular one, to which he aspired probably more than to the other.

We have said that in their totality the *Doine* represent an absolute novelty in the poetry of the period. The impact they made should have immediately started a great literary revolution; they would have done so if from the beginning they had been issued in a volume. It is a pity that conditions in Moldavia did not permit such a luxury. Printed separately at intervals, the poems seem to have surprised and embarrassed his contemporaries, at least at first. Accustomed to reading rooms where they could find only French books and reviews, so much local color was calculated to startle them. This strictly peasant poetry appeared to them humble and without prospects. In a way, they were right. Rumanian culture was not at that moment searching for nationalist isolation but for European and universal contacts, of which it had a vital need. But universality is the sum of total individualities, and Rumanian literature had first to be Rumanian. This ampler vision was reserved for a few enlightened minds, and these instantly approved the direction chosen by the poet. The latter confesses that the first inducement and the most precious one had come to him from Elena Negri and that it was for her sake that he became a popular poet.

In any case, the initial reserve did not last. The *Doine* in fact enjoyed a warm welcome among the Rumanian public, and their literary destiny was of the luckiest. The mark they left on Rumanian literature is important, perhaps even more so than on the work of Alecsandri itself, which quickly advanced toward other horizons. The poet went his way, while *Doine* had acquired a life of their own.

Translated into French by Ion Voinescu (1853) and partly into

English by Henry Stanley (1856) they helped—as *Poesii populare* had done—to make Rumanian literature known to Europe.[6] Internally, they gave rise to too extensive imitation that repeated to satiety the artificially idyllic aspects of rustic life, the idealized beauty of outlawry, and the glory of the past. Yet at the same time they exercised a salutary influence: the halting versification of Gypsy fiddlers' songs was quickly and radically condemned as soon as the new mode of popular verse, simple and crystal clear, had made its appearance. The *Doine* not only caused a stylistic clarification but also a permanent association of popular manner with great poetry; and the alliance between folkloric and romantic motifs perceived in *Ursiţii* and *Sburătorul* led up to Eminescu's *Luceafărul* (The Evening Star).

II. Lăcrămioare *(Lilies of the Valley)*

The second cycle of Alecsandri's poems is a return in time. First published in 1853, in the same volume as the first edition of *Doine,* it consists of twenty-two poems written between 1845 and 1847. Only three of the poems are of a later date—*Steluţa* (The Star), *Ursita mea* (My Destined Bride), *La Veneţia mult duioasă* (To Melancholy Venice)—but they are linked by their subject to the general theme of the cycle and together with them make a perfect unity.

Even the period when they were written shows that these poems date back to the time of his liaison with Elena Negri. All the poems in the cycle are devoted to this and are clearly lyrical autobiography. *Lăcrămioare* is, consequently, the poetical history of this love. Alecsandri had met Elena Negri in 1840, but the beginning of their liaison has been indicated by the poet with all the precision one could desire in the title of one of the poems *8 Mart* (March 8) (1845) in which he sings with an eloquence and spontaneity unequaled in other pieces of the cycle of the happiness of knowing himself loved. *De crezi în poezie* (If You Believe in Poetry), *O noapte la ţară* (A Night in the Country), and *Vezi tu vulturul* (See You the Eagle?) sing the plenitude of satisfied passion.

But after this first period of euphoria, their passion suffered some reverses on account of Elena's health and also because society watched them suspiciously. They therefore decided to avoid the public eye—*Despărţirea* (The Parting)—Elena going to look after her health in the West, and Alecsandri taking another route, through

Turkey; but their plan was to meet in Venice. Both the romantic reputation of this city of the lagoons and the memory of Alfred de Musset's lamentable adventure counted in this choice.[7] On the long road to this meeting, the poet did not cease to think of Elena—*Dulce înger* (Sweet Angel), *Cîntic de fericire* (Song of Happiness), *Așteptarea* (Expectation)—and only rarely had time to look for subjects from which she is absent *(Pescarul Bosforului)* (The Fisherman of the Bosporus).

In Venice the two lovers knew a few weeks of happiness that are recorded directly—*Veneția, O seară la Lido* (An Evening at the Lido), *Gondoleta* (The Gondola)—or indirectly—*Barcarola venețiana* (Venetian Barcarolle), *Biondineta*—in the verses of the collection When in Naples, they had not yet forgotten what happiness meant, although it already looked to them like a precarious oasis in the middle of a tempest *(Canțoneta napolitană)* (Neapolitan Song); and in Palermo happiness is only a distant dream *(Visurile)* (Dreams). Finally, the idyll comes to an end with Elena's death—*Adio* (Farewell), *Pe marea* (On the Sea)—and the poet is left with nothing but nostalgic mourning for lost delights—*Steluța* (The Little Star), *Ursita mea* (My Destined Bride), *La Veneția mult duioasă* (To Melancholy Venice).

In fact, then, *Lăcrămioare* is a diary of the poet's love—a verse diary parallel to the French account of the Italian journey which is a diary in prose. The documents are complementary, and quite surprisingly so, for such confessions in duplicate are not frequent in romantic poetry. What may be criticized in these verses is precisely their lack of polish and of poetical transfiguration; it is as if the poet were not writing for himself, and even less for a possible reader, but exclusively for Elena. For instance, in the middle of the beautiful outburst of feeling, in *8 Mart,* there is mention of a ride on horseback or the memory of the mother recently lost, which are faithful transcriptions of real experience but rouse no emotion in a third party. It is as if Alecsandri was writing so that he could read aloud to Elena all the declarations of love that their skepticism, or at least their fastidiousness, prevented them from telling one another directly.

The autobiographical character and the transparency of the allusions and names were so obvious that the poet hesitated when six years later he thought of publishing these verses. Costache Negri, Elena's brother, encouraged him and in a way gave him free hand. But even then, the poet did not come to a decision without once again consulting his old friend Kogălniceanu, text in hand, undoubtedly fearing the possible unpleasant comments about Elena that those ardent confessions might excite. [8]

The poetical interest of the cycle is very unequal. Such a total and immediate confession on the part of a man who always disliked to commit himself or dramatize and exaggerate his feelings could produce merely superficial unity, difficult to judge as a whole. The reasons are obvious. In the first place, in order to raise his poetical inspiration to the height of elegy, the poet deliberately abandoned the popular form in which he had shown such dexterity and launched into the commonplace metrics of anacreontic preromanticism and romantic declamation of the Lamartinean type, which reveal the triteness of the contents. As long as he was happy, the tone is satisfying and the declamation bearable; but his laments are far below the level of the feelings they claim to express. The principal cause of this failure is the poet's refusal to scrutinize himself and probe his feelings in depth. His confessions in prose are much more sincere and more eloquent than his artificial meditations in verse.

In the French diary, Alecsandri knows and admits that there could be no dream of love more beautiful than theirs. Yet it was a love that had no need of a Venetian setting; controlled and dignified, it was the love of aristocrats whose first thought was of decency and decorum, who hate romantic exaltation and theatrical passion. That is how Alecsandri must have been, and that is how we are bound to imagine Elena. It is probable that the only way they ever told one another how much they cared was by Alecsandri's artificial verses. This reserve, this critical spirit and lucidity is creditable, but it does not make poets: it is intelligible in Benjamin Constant but not in Lamartine. That is why the document in French prose is a first-class romantic confession of rare human insight, which would certainly have been envied by Stendhal had he known of it, while the verses which reflect exactly the same circumstances are powdered grimaces. Even Antonio, the hired gondolier, is more alive, more human, more artistically portrayed in the diary than is the kindly and diaphanous Tonio of *Biondineta* and *Gondoleta*.

Lăcrămioare, then, are the confessions of a lover who refused to confess. Hence the awkwardness of expression, under the surface of which we might never have guessed how strong and decisive was this love, were it not for the diary. From the point of view of Alecsandri's achievement as a poet, we see no progress; on the contrary, these lyrics, though written at the same time as the *Doine,* are a step back.

Yet what saves the collection as a whole and helped to ensure it an immediate and genuine success if not a lasting one is the new musicality of Alecsandri's verse. Trained in the school of Lamartine —an apprenticeship visible in almost all the verses of fourteen syllables—Alecsandri also repeats the patterns which he himself had earlier employed in his French verses. His craftsmanship is finer than the poetical expression of his feeling. The verse has a sonority, a vitality, a fluidity, and an abundance which Rumanian verse had never had before, and which Alecsandri had not even dreamed of in his first *Doine.* The content is in general confined to romantic commonplaces, but their sonorous elegance disguises the awkwardness of the elocution and the poverty of the images. For the first time Rumanian poetry succeeded in singing without the aid of a fiddle; no small triumph, and one which Eminescu was to use to such advantage.

A second merit is that in singing of his passion Alecsandri introduced a new decor into Rumanian poetry. The Orient and the glory of Italian landscape are glimpsed in passing, or are treated for the first time as poetical themes. Not insistently enough, for the poet is too exclusively preoccupied with his love; but it was on this new string that Alecsandri was later to harp.

III Suvenire *(Memories)*

Alecsandri's first collection of verse was the work of an enthusiast; the second, that of a lover. It may be said that *Suvenire,* the third in chronological order, is the work of a professional writer.

It is composed of two distinct series of verses, which need not have been brought together. Poems written between 1843 and 1846 figure in the first series although they might equally well have been included in the first cycle; but this inclusion would have damaged the inner unity of *Doine.* The poems written before 1846—*Visul* (The Dream), *Păsărica* (The Bird), *Maiorul Iancu Bran* (Major I. B.), *Desrobirea țiganilor* (The Emancipation of the Gypsies), *Odă către Bahlui* (Ode to Bahlui), *Zimbrul și vulpea* (The Bison and the Fox), *Curcile* (The Turkey-hens), *Adevărul și minciuna* (Truth and Falsehood), *Pe un album* (In an Album), *Bosforul* (The Bosphorus)—and which in consequence chronologically belong to the first cycle, have no relation whatever to the popular inspiration and meter predominant in the *Doine*. This fact leads us to suppose that the poet consciously eliminated them from the collection in order to preserve its unity but later found a place for them in this section as in a sort of appendix or supplement. The other poems, written after 1848 and before 1852, are ephemeral patriotic verses—*Adio Moldovei* (Farewell to Moldavia), *Intoarcere în ţară* (Return to My Country)—or are dedicated to friendship—*Strofe lui Costache Negri* (Verses to C. N.)—or to the memory of a recently deceased friend—*La mormîntul lui Grigore Romalo* (At the Tomb of G. R.), *La mormîntul lui P. Cazimir* (At the Tomb of P. C.), *Umbra lui Nicu Ghica* (The Shade of Nicu Ghica); only rarely does he sing of intimate lyrical feelings—*Romanţa* (Romance), *Dor de călătorie* (Longing for Travel)—or the smiling recollection of a recent idyll, *Dridri*.

The composite character of the collection is fairly obvious. Though many of the poems are devoted to memories, their number is not great enough to justify the title of the collection. The title is more probably to be explained as implying a comparison to the turning over of the leaves of an album. In any case, the variety of the themes seems to show that the author did not intend the same unity as in the previous collections and was content to assemble the *disjecta membra* that could not be inserted elsewhere. As *Suvenire* do not form a separate volume, we should consider them as a supplement so strictly subordinate to the principal cycle in the volume of 1853 that their title does not even appear on the cover.

However, the title of *Suvenire* is not wholly out of place. The dominant note is that of a nostalgic evocation of the past quite surprising in a young and optimistic poet like Alecsandri. In some of the poems we even perceive signs of an investigation into life's problems, and we can only regret he did not continue. We can guess that in his early years the poet was feeling his way in several different directions at the same time. The success of *Doine,* his continuous preoccupation with popular poetry, and perhaps suggestions from Elena soon decided his vocation. It is regrettable that he abandoned some directions in which his contribution might yet have been at least as useful to his reputation as a poet if not as fruitful in terms of the history of culture.

Visul, a poem written in 1843, is the first attempt at a Rumanian philosophical poem in this period. It is no doubt a cheap philosophy, which can be reduced to the ancient *vanitas vanitatum,* but which is nonetheless remarkable if we bear in mind the novelty of the theme at the date it was published and its uniqueness in Alecsandri's work. The same may be said of *Pe malul mării* (On the Sea Shore), the only poem in which the author shows himself as somberly tormented as a Byronic hero, seeking the sinister seascape of unchained breakers and a dull sky in order to feel more deeply the hopeless pain of losing his mother. These two poems are rare flowers in the whole of Alecsandri's works and give a totally unexpected image of the poet he might have been had he gone on trying to realize his inner self in poetry, instead of persistently drawing his poetry from externals.

The nostalgic echoes are multiplied whenever the poet comes across the grave of one of his recently deceased friends: Major Iancu Bran;[9] Grigore Romalo, the young revolutionary of 1848, who died after having been deported to Constantinople; Petru Cazimir, another 1848 comrade; Nicolae Ghica; and the strange and attractive figure of the Parisian actress Dridri, whose memory has all the nostalgic and sadly smiling charm of a flower pressed between the old pages of a forgotten book. It is not the evocation of Elena's unfading image among this slow dance of memories in *Strofe lui Costache Negri* that is surprising but the fact that the poet did not include these verses in *Lăcrămioare.* Perhaps he still nourished the illusion that nobody would discover the true identity of his lost beloved.

This collection also includes the few fables that Alecsandri wrote. This genre, completely outdated in the eyes of the romantics, had nonetheless taken a new lease on life in Rumanian literature during the first half of the nineteenth century because it was the only means of infiltrating political satire by cautiously wrapping it up in veils of allegory: for the poets of the period, fables took the place of Barbier's satire and the epigrammatic sting of Béranger. Alecsandri made use of it *(Păsărica, Zimbrul și vulpea)* to denounce Russian political pressures, somewhat as his contemporaries were doing in Wallachia. But in *Curcile* the fable is used for personal satire, the poet aspiring only to take revenge for some drawing-room gossip, perhaps regarding his idyll with Elena, and in *Odă către Bahlui* (which is not an ode in the lyrical sense) the satire is directed against poets unworthy of Castalia's pure waters whom we can no longer identify today.

Finally, contemporary politics also find a place among the poet's preoccupations—modest place as yet, for the only such composition is *Desrobirea ţiganilor*. In *Adio Moldovei* and *Intoarcerea în ţară* political passion blends with the same nostalgic feeling which is the keynote of the whole collection. It will be different in the following cycles in which the poet will strike the attitude of a bard.

IV Mărgăritărele *(Lilies of the Valley)*

The cycle of poems entitled *Mărgăritărele* was published in 1863 as a supplement to the second edition of the volume *Doine şi lăcrămioare*. It consists of forty-six poems written almost wholly during the years 1852–62; four of them date from an earlier period (1843–48), and these were not included in the edition of 1853, doubtless for political reasons.

The extreme dates of the collection show that, from the point of view of chronology, it is a direct continuation of *Suvenire;* it represents no unitary inspiration or selective effort but is nearly the poet's entire output over a series of years. This is reflected also in the contents which are at least as varied as those of the preceding collection.

The title does not seem particularly appropriate, perhaps because we miss the point of it. *Mărgăritărele* is a second name for *lăcrămioare* (lilies of the valley), flowers that furnished the title for one of the preceding series. But it is difficult to say if the poet thought of establishing any symbolic connection between them. A connection with the title of the last poem in this cycle, *Inşiră-te mărgărite* (Be Threaded, Pearl), has been proposed, but this is doubtful, for the likeness between *mărgărite* (pearls) and *mărgăritărele* (flowers) is deceptive. The romantic fashion for keepsakes, with their flowery borders, and the success of some collections of verses bearing similar titles, as for instance *Myosotis* by Hégésippe Moreau, may have influenced this choice of flower names for titles. But the most plausible explanation of all seems to be that the poet intended to pay homage—in a way at once secret and transparent—to the woman who inspired him with the love he celebrates in many poems of this cycle, and whom he calls Mărgărita.

It is obvious that the idea of a keepsake or souvenir album was present to the poet's imagination; as in *Suvenire* the stress is on the autobiographical poems. In *Păsărica mărei* (The Bird of the

Sea), the bird which tells sailors that land is somewhere near, is compared to the secret voice of love promising happiness and also to the voice of freedom promising his country a glorious future— a double polarity of lyrical inspiration to which Alecsandri is beginning to accustom us. *Floarea oceanului* (The Flower of the Ocean), the flower which blooms on sheer cliffs threatened by the breakers, is the tender memory of the beloved calling from afar, shining in the darkness like the flash of a lighthouse. Both these little poems are peculiarly characteristic; they reveal in Alecsandri a sort of interpenetration with the French poetry of the period in its more novel aspects. Thus, they form a sort of prehistoric age of Rumanian symbolism, although we cannot establish clearly whether it is a case of conscious experiment or mere coincidence.

Although it is not clear who was the beloved alluded to it was probably the mysterious Mărgărita whom he praised in other compositions of this cycle and about whom we know nothing at all. Other poems seem to belong to the same episode, although the allusions are not too clear. In *Vis de poet* (Poet's Dream), first entitled *Mărgărita,* in which the woman he loves expresses her bliss in the knowledge that she inspires him to sing both his love for her and his love for his country, he employs terms and ideas that are close both to the twofold program of *Păsărica mărei* and to suggestions made to him thirteen years before by Elena Negri. In *Cîntice și sărutări* (Songs and Kisses) the same dialogue is taken up again. *Iachtul* (The Yacht) is another travel poem, in which the memory of his beloved with the flower name accompanies him through Spain. *Stele* (Stars) is an odd *doină* written in Seville, and the stars of which he sings are two tears of joy. *Intîi Mai* (May 1) is the first date in the lover's calendar, as *Adio* is the final point of this mysterious idyl, in which the name of the protagonist is missing but which can be reconstructed without much difficulty by allusions in these compositions and by the biographical details to be found in the short story *Mărgărita*. All these poems form the emotional nucleus of the collection and thus explain the title chosen by the poet. His inconstant heart seems to have completely forgotten Elena; and if so, the precise parallelism of the title *Mărgărițărele* and that of *Lăcrămioare* shows a certain irreverence.

It is not easy to explain the exact meaning of this inspiration, given our total ignorance of the circumstances to which it refers. The poet seems unaware of betraying a hallowed memory; in fact, Elena's memory is vaguely present. In *Dorul de mare* (Yearning for the Sea), the journey he is dreaming of is not to new horizons but one that would lead him on a retrospective pilgrimage, through the Bosporus to Venice, Naples, and Palermo, as it had done in the times of his great, but momentary, happiness. In *Gondola trece* (The Gondola Passes), the picture of Venice is no longer the swift vision of old but the icy consciousness that all is ended and that life will not begin again.

It is, after all, possible that there is no inconstancy or betrayal in this apparent duplicity. The idyll with Margarita may well be less real than we imagine, and Alecsandri may have poured into it many of the old memories connected with Elena. This would explain not only the obvious parallelism of the two cycles but also the less vivid impression made by the feelings there expressed. We do not mean by this that Margarita never existed; but the interpretation of the episode is no longer so immediate and precise as in *Lăcrămioare* and seems filtered through old memories and emotions. A proof of this would be the relative incongruity of the version in *Adio,* where it is a question of a commonplace separation between two lovers who are aware that their idyll can no longer endure— exactly as in the story *Mărgărita*—with that in *Vis de poet,* where the beloved has, like the dream, flown to heaven—exactly as in *Steluţa.* There may have been two quite different idylls, for poets' hearts are capacious; but we should not forget that their imagination is equally so.

Other pages in this keepsake are travel sketches and refer to his journeys through Spain—*O noapte la Alhambra* (A Night at Alhambra), *Şeguidilă* (Seguidilla), *El R'Baa* (The Arab Steed)—and through Italy—*Presimţire* (Presentiment), *Pe albumul d-rei Ida Vegezzi-Ruscalla* (In the Album of Miss I.V.-R.), *Pilotul* (The Pilot), *La Palestro* (At Palestro), *La Magenta* (At Magenta), *Lacul de Como* (Lake Como), and a trilogy devoted to the battle of Solferino *Coroana vieţei* (The Crown of Life). In the verses belonging to the first series the interest of the composition lies in the picturesque notation and a rather superficial exoticism, learned from Victor Hugo's *Orientales* rather than from contemplation of Andalusian landscape. In the other series, contemporary history is more deeply felt than the geographical framework. The poet sings of the warlike effort of the young Italian kingdom, for in it he sees a prefiguration of the future Rumanian effort to live an independent

national life. The above-named poems might in a way serve as preface to *Ostașii noștri*.

Like pages of an album, too, are the poems which, as in the
preceding cycle, mourn for the recent loss of a dear one: *Nicolae
Bălcescu murind* (N. B. Dying); *Emmi*, an elegy on the death of
a young girl, which probably sounded in the ears of Eminescu when
he was writing *Mortua est* (She is Dead); *Surorii mele* (To my Sister),
an elegy dedicated to the memory of Catinca Rolla, which was soon
to become a popular romance.

Among the poems that from a chronological point of view do
not belong to the cycle *Mărgăritărele*, the oldest is *Muntele de foc*
(The Mountain of Fire). It was first published in 1843 in the prose
tale *Suvenire din Italia* and inserted with it in *Călătorie în Africa*
(1855). The year 1840 is generally suggested as the date of its
composition;[11] but at that period Alecsandri does not seem to
have been able to write Rumanian verses, and there are no
adequate grounds for this dating. Whether it be 1840 or, as is more
probable, 1843, it is certain that we have here a composition over-
looked by the poet in the volume of 1853, for otherwise its publication here would not be justified.

The case of the other older poems appears to be somewhat different since they are patriotic and revolutionary and would have
passed the censorship in 1853 with difficulty. *Deșteptarea României*
(The Awakening of Rumania) had been published on handbills in
1848, the year when it was composed in order to incite the struggle
for liberty and national unity. It was in its time a kind of *Marseil-
laise* of the national movement and one of the most popular among
Alecsandri's poems—quite rightly so, for once—for it is written
with an impetus and a warmth not found in all of Alecsandri's
patriotic inspirations.

Sentinela română (The Rumanian Sentry), a historical poem,
dates from about the same period and was published for the first
time in *România literară* of 1855. In it the meter of popular ballads
is rather cunningly blended with the idea so precious to Transylvanian Latinists, which Alecsandri borrowed from them, of the
descent of Rumanians from Rome, of their continuity on Dacian
soil, and of their certainty of a brilliant future which follows with the
logic of a mathematical corollary from this attractive premise. The
poem is below the level of Alecsandri's art as we have seen it applied
to other poems in popular meters; this is not surprising, for the theme

is a new one and does not fit in with traditional verse and the structure of the poem shows it to be mere improvisation. Yet the stir caused by this poem was great, especially in Transylvania where it so well answered the need of the moment and the general trend of Rumanian culture. *Moțul și Secuiul* (The Motz and the Szekely), a revolutionary and warlike song, dates from the same time.

A similar patriotic chord vibrates in other parts of the collection. Sometimes, in accordance with the program already mentioned, the call of history is united to the finer and sweeter voice of love— *Vis de poet* (Poet's Dream), *Cîntice și sărutări* (Songs and Kisses). At other times the historical explosion is caused directly by current events, in which the poet had taken such an active part. Among these last compositions we must mention *Anul 1855* (The Year 1855), in which, partly imitating *Anul 1840* (The Year 1840), the poem of his Wallachian friend Grigore Alexandrescu, he sings of the new hopes and illusions brought about by the European situation; *La Sevastopol* (At Sevastopol), in which the bloody spectacle of the war yet permits—exactly as in Italy during the same years—hope of a better future for the poet's country; *Moldova în 1857* (Moldavia in 1857), which is a vehement diatribe, in a violent language most unusual to Alecsandri, against politicians who endeavored to oppose the impetuous movement that was leading to the union, because their own interests were in conflict with the national interest; *Steaua țării* (The Star of the Land), dating from the same period, and the famous *Hora Unirii* (1857), the historical merit of which far transcends the literary.

Finally, a last series of poems belonging to this cycle comes naturally as a continuation of *Doine*. Chronologically, this continuity is not surprising, as we have already seen that the last *doine* were from 1852; *Mărgăritărele* resumes the interrupted thread taking it on to 1862. This is the perspective in which the compositions that seem to prolong the series of popular ballads should be understood.

In *Biserica risipită* (The Ruined Church) the phantasmagoric effect and the satanism of *Strigoiul* are combined with a more or less authentic local tradition, exactly as in the earlier examples of *Erculean* and *Maghiara*. *Hoțul și Domnița* (The Robber and the Princess) is a mere replica of *Sora și Hoțul* (The Nun and the Robber) in *Doine*. *Dragoș* and *Visul lui Petru Rareș* (P. R.'s Dream) are legends by which Alecsandri aims at completing missing traditions as he had many times done in *Poesii populare*. As a matter of fact, the poem *Dragoş* was later included in the collection *Poesii populare,* thus constituting the odd and unique example of a poem figuring in two concomitantly. In *Cîntice de lume* (Worldly Songs), the authentic popular verses are intertwined with those of Alecsandri. *Inşiră-te Mărgărite,* which concludes the cycle of *Mărgăritărele,* exactly as *Marioara Florioara* formed a kind of finale to *Doine,* is a fairly successful versification of a folklore motif and pairs with the above-mentioned fairy tale. Finally, *Banul Mărăcine* is the strangest of all the so-called popular ballads of Alecsandri, for, in the guise of an old song, it enacts a false tradition that is not even Rumanian, that of the Rumanian origin of the French poet Ronsard's ancestors. This alleged tradition starts from Ronsard's assertion that the origins of his family are to be sought in Thrace and the Danube Valley; one must not, of course, take seriously such humanistic fantasies, to which the French poet resorted because he liked to consider himself a compatriot of Orpheus. Inspired by this assertion the French teacher Vaillant, who taught for several years in Bucharest, made Ronsard descend from a nonexistent *ban* (governor) of Oltenia, called Mărăcine, which is merely the translation of the French poet's name into Rumanian;[12] it was from Vaillant that Alecsandri borrowed this "tradition."[13] From Alecsandri's point of view it is not difficult to understand that the theme was exceptionally interesting sentimentally and as propaganda. Like many other falsely "popular" productions of Alecsandri, this legend has become popular and is even sung and danced in certain rural circles.

Situated as it is midway in its author's life, *Mărgăritărele* is only a doubtful success. Doubt is, in fact, the dominant note of this cycle. With *Doine* Alecsandri had opened up a very new and personal path that, here too, he follows with the same ability, but not with the same constancy. The elegiac tone of *Lăcrămioare* is taken up again, not without some faint indications of a parallelism which we do not rightly understand; at the same time, as in *Suvenire,* contemporary affairs keep breaking in.

In the cycle *Suvenire,* the poem *Visul* appeared as a sort of programmatic preface in which imagination proposed to the poet the threefold temptation of pleasure, glory, and love. In *Mărgăritărele,* the real preface is the poem *Vis de poet,* in which the woman he loves urges the poet to sing of his emotions but without forgetting

that his country also needs his voice. In both cycles it is obvious
that the poet is distracted and that the road no longer seems to him
as definite and clear as in *Doine*.[14]

V Pasteluri *(Pastels)*

The collection entitled *Pasteluri* is composed of forty poems,
the majority of which were published for the first time in the review
Convorbiri literare during the years 1868–74 and were collected
for the first time in volume III of *Opere complete*. The date *1862—
7* . . . as a subtitle shows that the author did not consider the cycle
as ended at the time of publication. *Suvenire* bore no chronological
indication in the title but represented the production of the years
1842–52; *Mărgăritărele,* that of 1852–62; and so *Pasteluri* directly
continued the preceding series, presenting another ten years of
poetical output.

Yet this regularity is only apparent. *Suvenire* did not bear any
indication of the years of its creation, nor did it claim to offer more
than part of the first period's production, as we already have seen
that it forms a collection contemporaneous with *Doine* and *Lăcrămioare*. On the other hand, *Pasteluri* does not actually cover the
years indicated. The majority of poems belonging to this cycle,
and in any case the most significant ones, are from 1867–69; and
when the poet decided to add earlier poems, they were not taken
from 1862 but were much earlier works. Consequently, there is a
certain artifice in the dates presented, which indicate intentions
rather than realities. The most probable of these intentions was a
desire for unity, which is also obvious in the contents.

Yet unity, as in the previous collections, is only partly achieved.
In fact, the authentic pastels are the first thirty poems; the others
belong to different dates, inspirations, and metrical forms and have
been added at the end of the collection in order to make up that full
measure which the poet felt he owed his readers.

On the other hand, the first thirty poems form a cycle that is
extremely compact and well organized but remains unfinished.
The poetical calendar of life at Mircești omits autumn. The poet
felt bound to complete it, which is why he left the final date open
(187 . . .), so as to reserve himself the possibility of taking this series
up again to round it off, though he never did this. As it has come to
us, the *Pasteluri* series is not only incomplete but seems somewhat

out of balance because of the excessive weight of the final additions, which spoil its unity.

The genesis of *Pasteluri* is explained by three circumstances which together determined Alecsandri's new poetical orientation. First of all, these poems were written at Mircești in a period when the poet had definitely opted for a quiet life in the countryside. Alecsandri was not made for introspection. His manner of life tended outward: when deprived of his previous themes (love, friendship, love of his country, exotic landscapes), the eyes of his poetry opened on surrounding nature. One notices even in his daily life that his new state of spirit was conditioned by Mircești. In his correspondence he often fixed something in the future, not by the calendar, but by the corresponding agricultural tasks. *Pasteluri* are not paintings from nature in general but the mirror of days at Mircești.

The idea of transforming a rather modest and dull setting into poetry is Alecsandri's great merit. He was, of course, helped by the example of contemporary French poetry. For treating landscape as adequate material in itself for poetry he had the example of the school of transition toward Parnassianism, led by Théophile Gautier and Théodore de Banville and, above all, the example of Leconte de Lisle, whose preoccupation with decor was, we presume, what familiarized Alecsandri with the idea that poetry is not only narrative and declamation, but up to a point, can be transformed into painting.

Finally, the third circumstance contributing to the relatively swift realization of this new poetical vision was the recent appearance of *Convorbiri literare*. Until that moment, Alecsandri's poetical production had not found a handy outlet; the reviews for which he had written were either too far away or had enjoyed too short an existence. But now, the friendly presence of *Convorbiri literare,* always ready and pleased to give his contribution a place of honor, was almost a guarantee of publication, so that Alecsandri, feeling an incentive, if not a moral obligation, to write, persevered with his plan—even if once again he did not bring it to completion. The plan, as we have already said, was to compile a calendar of life at Mircești. The poet proposed to sing methodically of all that made up the specific life of his house, the village, the fields, and the meadow, from one "End of Autumn" to another. And this is in fact how he carried it out. Winter (poems III–X), spring (XI–XXIV), and summer (XXV–XXX) are comprehensively depicted in their various aspects; but Alecsandri stopped too soon. Summer and autumn are not sufficiently represented compared to the other seasons, autumn, in fact, being practically omitted. The otherwise perfect division of the poetic year proves that there is no question of random inspiration but of a carefully planned project.

This lack of spontaneity does not augur well. Nevertheless, *Pasteluri* is undoubtedly the most successful, the most attractive, and the most sincere part of all Alecsandri's poetical work. The success is to be explained by the happy choice of the general tonality, which for the first time is in agreement with his temperament. In other words, the romantic who was fleeing from romanticism, the lyric poet who hated confessions, was by vocation a Parnassian. Alecsandri had no means of knowing this in 1853, and he may not have entirely realized it even during the years when he was writing *Pasteluri*. Alecsandri's dreams were not of marble like Leconte de Lisle's; he merely toyed now and then with enamel, like Gautier. All in all, his technique and emotional camouflage are very happily expressed by the title *Pasteluri:* he could as well have called them water colors or gouaches. In fact, this collection resembles not so much an album of objective photographs as an autobiographical film, in which the director is at the same time the chief actor, though stylishly he never shows himself in the foreground.

This does not mean that he is absent for one moment. On the contrary, the decor is mere decor, subordinated to the process of revealing the author and his state of spirit. It is the poet who becomes pensive in *Sfîrșit de toamnă* (End of Autumn), who amorously sits close in *Sania* (The Sleigh) or contemplates phantoms and imaginary beauties in *La gura sobei* (At the Mouth of the Stove). It is he who envies migratory birds because they have seen horizons unattainable by him—the Nile and the mountains of the moon, Kashmire and Ceylon.

If it is true that the landscape painter is never objective, it is even more true of the descriptive poet. In the present instance, Alecsandri is not only the eye that sees; he is also the eye which watches itself seeing. Through landscape, Alecsandri indirectly reveals himself, speaks without his customary reserve and self-dissimulation, conceives of himself as an object. This had rarely happened before. In this way, the poet who has never been sincere with himself becomes so at last, for he thinks he is talking about something outside himself. It is only thus that we are able to surprise him, and we are faced with the paradox that we do not know and do not appreciate Alecsandri as a lyrical poet except through his descriptions.

It is, consequently, not surprising that his most perfect achievements are in *Pasteluri*. Among them, the first poem which serves as a preface to the whole collection is perhaps his poetical masterpiece. In *Serile la Mircești* (Evenings at Mircești) it is winter, and the poet is languishing in the indoor warmth. He is dreaming, smoking, lazily gazing at the pictures adorning the walls: an odalisque, a battlefield, a view of Venice. Suddenly these dead landscapes come alive and arouse that periodical nostalgia for travel that comes to him together with winter and cold, year by year. He then sets off through the transparent smoke of his cigarette on his journey into imagination and memories, through familiar islands and seas, through exotic landscapes splendidly described as fleeting visions. Traveling in space turns into a return in time, a portrait recalls to him his dead love and—a superb expression Alecsandri was never to achieve again—"the happy time of suffering." All is now ashes and smoke, nostalgia and loneliness. It is cold and it is dark, but the poet is at peace with himself: there is no rebellion against the consciousness of the gloom that envelops him because, to anyone familiar with the study of seasons, there can be no surprise in the prospect of winter and of the end lying in wait for us.

To begin with, this journey around his room, from which the memory of Xavier de Maistre is not wholly absent, is a moral portrait of the author. An artful portrait, it is only tangentially presented, if not with its back to its object, looking or pretending to make us look at the pictures on the wall and the smoke that curls up from the cigarette. Alecsandri's physiological sensibility, so much affected by the cold; his psychology, that of a man in love with light and sun, his predilection for superficial intermittent dreaming, made up rather of visions than meditations—all these traits of character are interpreted by the complete interpenetration of the man and his setting. There is so little searching for effect that the poem would lose practically nothing if it were turned into prose. Nevertheless, the poetic diction itself has attained such a maturity and such exceptional fluency that its lack of artifice intensifies the initial impression of an intimate confession. But the great merit of the composition lies in the continuous blending of what is seen with what is imagined of the cigarette smoke and the radiant landscapes where towns and fairies float, of the past and the present, of suffering and happiness. Alecsandri never attained a higher level of art or of sincerity, or perhaps of both at once; two or three more such poems would suffice to refute what we have said above—that Alecsandri was not born a poet.

The theme of imagination conceived as the only faculty to remain lively during the winter evenings recurs in *La gura sobei*. This time it is not so successfully put across: in the flames of the hearth the poet no longer contemplates his own existence but discovers and relives popular tales. In *Malul Siretului* (The Bank of the Siret) his thoughts glide along with the river towards unseen, mysterious distances. But the power of concentration is no longer the same, for the meadow itself is too near an object, too full of life, and distracts the poet's attention from the evocation of unknown horizons toward which the water is flowing.

On the whole, the poet's attitude as an active personage and a living element in the picture is not resolved into pure contemplation. For him temptations are mainly of a social kind, as might have been expected. He is attracted by the presence of people; they are his chief interest. The drive with the woman he loves in *Sania* transforms the monotonous landscape into a pleasant and positive setting. *Puntea* (The Bridge), *Fîntîna* (The Well), *Secerişul* (The Reaping) or *Cositul* (The Mowing) are more idyls than purely descriptive poems.

The same might be said of many other pastels in which the natural setting is of less interest to the poet than the people who bring life into it. In *Paştele* (Easter) all is bustle; in *Plugurile* (The Plows), in *Semănătorii* (The Sowers), and in *Rodica,* the laborers occupy the whole horizon; little is seen but their specific activity, so that their intervention creates a sort of animated landscape. In all these compositions the rural atmosphere is that imagined by Alecsandri and reproduced by him in poetry as well as in the theater: a joyous peasantry, happy and with no problems, ready for a joke, as fictitious as that in eighteenth-century pastorals. Its favorite language seems to be song, and the ritual gestures of toil give no sense of the arduous or mechanical, resembling rather the steps of a ballet. Alecsandri has been bitterly reproached for this lack of realism, and we shall not dwell upon it here; but we might as easily reproach his critics for requiring realistic descriptions from a poet who held strictly idealistic conceptions and who adorned and embellished not only the peasantry but all the subjects he chose or imagined.

The same bustle that appears in the pastels animated by the pre-

sence of people is also to be found in those from which man is
absent. This effect is sometimes obtained by personifications, as
in *Gerul* (The Frost), or by dynamic representations, where every
detail of the picture intervenes as an active element. Thus it is in
Dimineaţa (Morning), where the picture is summoned up by characteristic activities: laborers preparing their tools, birds clearing
their throats, fires burning, cattle lowing. Another characteristic
example of the activation of the natural setting is *Lunca din Mirceşti* (The Meadow at Mirceşti), seen in May, in the full effervescence of spring: everything is pulsing with new life, the oak is
talking to the grass, the butterfly to the flower, and even the eagle to
the nightingale, for all has to be dualism and pairing; the meadow
resembles a garden of Armida, a nest of love where everything
expresses the joy of living. The poem is well constructed too, although with some affectation that goes beyond the intimate intentions and the general tone of the cycle; the artifice not only
reduces our belief in its sincerity, it also turns the author from a
spectator into a wizard. That may also be said of *Concertul în
luncă* (Concert in the Meadow), a bravura piece which certainly
was inspired by the concert in the same garden of Armida in Tasso's
famous poem; all the flowers, birds, and insects meet to listen to
the song of the nightingale, which is conceived as a sample of virtuosity, a sort of violin solo in the midst of a concert.[15]

Finally, when the presence of swarming crowds or the activation
of natural elements is deemed inopportune, a ray of light, a musical
note is sufficient to animate the surroundings: for example, the
joyous tinkling of the bells adding their final note, so fresh and
unexpected, in *Iarna* (Winter) and transforming the dreary landscape into a kind of oasis; or in *Viscolul* (The Blizzard) the prospect
of the cottage's lighted window which is seen from afar and casts
a patch of light in a picture all darkness and menace. The strokes
of light are numerous and precise in *Sfîrşitul iernii* (The End of
Winter) and mingle with those of sound in *Noaptea* (Night), where
the falling stars and the fires on the hills are associated with the
sound of the *bucium* (alpenhorn), the barking of dogs and the
chorus of frogs, to suggest animation where one would expect
silence and immobility.

The heterogeneous poems annexed to the cycle *Pasteluri,* although unconnected with the poetical calendar of Mirceşti, have a
family likeness to the descriptive themes already analyzed. The

two *Portrete* (Portraits), one written in 1868 and the other written about 1855, were published side by side because they are constructed according to the laws of counterpoint, the first dedicated to a cold and distant beauty who freezes her would-be lover, while the second woman, more attractive than beautiful, instantly inspires sympathy and adoration. *Pe coastele Calabriei* (On the Shores of Calabria) recalls the former Italian landscapes sung in earlier cycles, and *Linda Raia,* which would have been more fittingly included in the Andalusian cycle of *Mărgăritărele,* has no visible connection with descriptive poetry; *Calea Robilor* (The Milky Way) takes us again to the pseudo-legendary inspiration of *Doine.*

More interesting are the last poems of the collection. *Mandarinul* (The Mandarin) and *Pastel chinez* (Chinese Pastel) are miniatures executed with infinite care for detail and with an art so precise and minute that it very much recalls Théophile Gautier. Both descriptions are inspired by some engraving if not by a Chinese screen. What probably interested Alecsandri in these subjects more than the multiplying of graceful diminutive detail was the problem of expression, inasmuch as exotic description, taken up again by Macedonski later, was a novelty in the poetry of his time. From this point of view, his twofold experiment is a success. The poems in themselves are strictly descriptive, and consequently we should not look for other qualities, but they attain a perfect elegance, precision, and fluency and are among Alecsandri's best exercises in versification. Finally, *Valul lui Traian* (Trajan's Wall), a composition that seems to be much older (if the suggested dating to 1844 is exact, though it seems doubtful), is another exercise in style. In it the intention to detail and enumerate is combined with that wish to acclimatize an exotic vocabulary which preoccupied the poet in the Chinese miniatures.

VI Legende *(Legends)*

This cycle, the most considerable in length, consists of thirty-two poems and was first published in a volume in 1875; it forms the second part of the volume of *Opere complete* in which *Pasteluri* also made its appearance. In this first edition only the first sixteen pieces of the series were included; its second half first appeared in the 1880 edition of *Opere complete,* where it forms the first part of volume III with the collective title of *Legende nouă* (New Legends).

In the meantime, with few exceptions, they had all in turn been published in *Convorbiri literare*. The composition of these poems dates from the years 1868–78, the only exception being *Tudora de la Tîrşor* (Tudora from Tîrşor) which is from 1864.

The collective title proves, as in the case of *Pasteluri* with which they coincide in time, a wish to offer a unitary collection of poems belonging to a single genre. In spite of that, as in previous cases, such unity is far from being achieved. There exists throughout the volume a permanent confusion of genres, which alone renders possible the presence of a romance like *Dorul de brazi* (Longing for Firs), of an ode like *Odă statuii lui Mihai Viteazu* (Ode to the Statue of M. V.), of *Cînticul gintei latine,* or of an elegy like *Strofe improvizate lui C. Rolla* (Impromptu Stanzas to C. R.).[16] As in earlier cases, it is difficult to imagine that the author was mistaken in his attempts to classify. We must rather admit that, from his point of view, the title of *Legende* aims only at suggesting the general tonality of the volume.

Confining ourselves for the present to the poems which correspond to the general title of the collection, the legends may be divided according to the material they refer to into historical and mythological groupings. The first treat subjects borrowed from national history or, more rarely, a few exotic subjects. The group of national legends is much more important and seem to indicate Alecsandri's wish to continue in new and more up-to-date forms his campaign to exploit the past, which he had initiated with *Doine* and the collection *Poesii populare*. The themes are indeed often similar; the styles, only occasionally. From popular ballads, he now aspired to the form of the epic. The line is almost everywhere that of fourteen syllables, which he had already employed, but its constant application makes the whole look like assembled fragments of a vast epic—a look that is, of course, not fortuitous.

What Alecsandri proposed was to give Rumanian literature the epic that it lacked.[17] His post-classical formation doubtless led him to consider the epic to be the highest form of poetic art, a preconception held by the first doctrinaire critics of the Renaissance and only partly uprooted by the romantic rebellion. He consequently endeavored, as his admired Voltaire had done before him, to endow his nation's poetry with the only genre it lacked. He would probably not have thought seriously of such a project, at a time when epics had been superseded by epic fiction in prose, had Victor Hugo not by his *Légende des Siècles* breathed new vigor into it. The first series of these poems, issued in 1859, bore the characteristic subtitle of *Histoire: les petites épopées,* indicating a new orientation more in accordance with the poetical tendencies of his time toward epic considered as an episodic and cyclic poem with its own development and more modest proportions, yet integrating itself into a vast ensemble.

This plan attracted Alecsandri, and his debt to Victor Hugo is obvious. The little epic—as the latter called it—is to be found at the basis of *Legende* and claims to bring back the past, not only as isolated moments in history, but also as steps in the national evolution. Optimism and faith in the religion of progress are part of Hugo's poetical vision as well as Alecsandri's. And even more than this similarity of conception, the details and technical procedure show that the example of Victor Hugo's French poems was constantly of help to Alecsandri.[18]

The differences are important, however. Alecsandri did not have the sap, the epic vigor, or the imagination of Hugo, and it would have been rash on his part to set himself like the French poet to sing the history of all mankind. His flight could not have taken him as high, and his problems had always been linked to his country's past and destiny rather than to the fate or evolution of mankind at large. His *Legende* are a sort of pocket edition of *La Légende des Siècles,* in which the dimensions have been reduced, both in terms of the number of verses and of the extent of the field of imagination. This proves that the poet knew himself well; his creative power had nothing titanic about it.

If we were to judge him more severely, we might say that in his new capacity as epic poet, in spite of Hugo's influence, Alecsandri did no more in *Legende* than he had done before: he transformed popular ballads into small epics. This last genre was not invented by Victor Hugo; it was just a revival on a larger scale of the historical ballad, as it had been practiced by the romantic school. The poems with Rumanian subjects in *Legende* are in this sense the result of a normal evolution. The only new idea was the inspiration which was to build them into great ensembles, an inspiration which remained more of an intention than a reality.

The first poem of the cycle is the most important: *Dumbrava Roşie* (The Red Grove) has 859 verses, divided into eight parts, and tells of the fight of Stephen the Great, prince of Moldavia, against John

Albert, king of Poland, in the year 1497; of the defeat of the Polish
army; and of the atrocious episode of the thousand Polish pri-
soners being yoked and made to plow and sow with acorns the hills
that were to be covered later by the forest which bears to this day
the name of Dumbrava Roşie.

This victory was a subject easy to exploit in the service of an
exacerbated patriotism of the romantic sort, where all that is
national is excellent, from the prince to the humblest peasant or
soldier, and where all that is foreign is bad. In accordance with this
convenient formula, the poet concocts the inconsistent character
of King John Albert in contrast with the heroic traits of the Moldavian prince. The whole composition is correct, but forced, and
what is lacking above all is the epic impetus that cannot be acquired
by artificial means.

In his characterizations, in the presentation of the two camps that
confront one another, Alecsandri partly makes use of *Cetatea
Neamţului* (The Citadel of Neamtz) by Costache Negruzzi, which
many years earlier he had turned into a national drama. The most
successful bravura piece of all is perhaps the speech of Stephen the
Great to his soldiers, constructed as it is on rhetorical principles
learned from Victor Hugo, but ably enough deployed and not
devoid of dramatic force and grandeur: one seems to see behind
the epic poet the playwright, who was soon to make his characters
from Rumanian history speak the same poetical language. Otherwise, the enumeration of the heroes in each camp, the spurious
abundance of names and their scanty characterization, and the description of the camps and the battlefield are academic composition,
as correct as they are lifeless: we seem to be watching Ingres painting
a battle scene.

Dan capitan de plai (Captain Dan) is similar up to a point. It
refers to the same Moldavian fifteenth century and to the periodic
fights between Rumanians and Tatars. The personages—the old
Captain Dan, the frontier guard Ursan and his daughter Fulga—
have no connection whatsoever with history. Ursan was introduced
here solely to associate Wallachia with this essay in epic, as the
author has taken care to inform us that this hero comes from the
other bank of the river Milcov. Fulga is a sort of Bradamante or
Clorinda, a direct descendant from Renaissance Italian epic, which
was well known to Alecsandri and appreciated by him. All in all,
the poem is more spontaneous and less forced because it is less

pretentious, reduced as it is to the scale of individual heroics and lesser events and encounters. *Dan* is the most popular of the legends in this cycle; its popularity is not enough to guarantee its absolute value, but is not unjustified.

The same series of adventures in connection with the frequent incursions by Tatar hordes furnish the subject of *Ana Doamna* (Princess Ana) and *Ghioaga lui Briar* (Briar's cudgel). The first is vaguely situated in the Middle Ages; the second at the time of Dragoş, the first prince of Moldavia. But the historical foundation is equally illusory in each. The one is concerned with the motherly love of Ana, who kills the Tatar khan to save her child; she is a sort of Andromache bent on defending herself with her own resources. The other tells of the extravagant adventure of Briar, famous only for his savagery and the exceptional size of his mace. We do not know where Alecsandri collected these subjects which, of course, have nothing to do with tradition. It is true that in *Dan căpitan de plai* he quotes as a motto a few so-called popular verses with the obvious intention of making us believe that the subject was already familiar from ballads. But the verses do not appear authentic, nor is the name of the person met with in ballads.

The same may be said of *Stroe Plopan,* which bears the subtitle of *Popular Ballad* and which is indeed the only legend in this cycle to be written in the rhythm of ancient songs. The subject is not much different from those examined above: Stroe saves from the hands of the Tatars a girl they had made their slave and then marries her. The poem does not bear any indication of date but is certainly linked with older customs, and we dare not be more precise, nor say whether it has any basis in tradition.

At other times the historical material is taken straight from texts. In *Calul Cardinalului Batori* (Cardinal Batori's Horse) the starting point is a text from the Greek chronicle of Stavrinos, while rhythm and style curiously enough come from Bolintineanu, himself an admirer and disciple of Alecsandri. *Tudora dela Tîrşor* (Tudora from Tîrşor), which is written in a meter very similar to the popular one and in which we may perceive the influence of historical ballads as conceived by German romantics, starts from a reference in the chronicle of Mihai Viteazul. In *Vlad Ţepeş şi stejarul* (V.Ţ. and the Oak) the source is again a chronicle, but there is a greater distance between the indications of the text and the poet's fancies. The other poems with Rumanian subjects in the cycle are com-

memorative: an *Odă statuii lui Mihai Viteazul* (Ode to the Statue
of M. V.), quite out of place in a collection of legends but probably
included as of historical interest; an eulogy of *Cuza Vodă,* equally
unsuited to such a context because it is, like *Strofe improvizate
la moartea lui C. Rolla* (Impromptu Stanzas on the Death of C. R.),
a memorial to the deceased friend at the date of his death; *La
răpirea Bucovinei* (On the Rape of Bucovina), written on the occasion of the commemorative ceremonies of 1875, the centenary
of the loss of this part of Moldavia.

Among the historical legends embroidered on material that does
not belong to the Rumanian past, three have grown out of Easter
surroundings. *Hodja Murad Paşa* (H. M. Pasha) tells how the
cruelty of a vizier who had ordered the death of a Christian babe,
was punished by the death of his three sons, and it includes quite
unexpectedly a pretty close imitation of Victor Hugo's poem
Aymerillot, that being, in fact, its chief interest. *Garda Saraiului*
(The Guard of the Seraglio) is an *Orientale* in which the accent is
placed on local color, the so-called historical anecdote presenting
little interest. Finally, *Murad Gazi Sultanul şi Becri Mustafa* (Sultan
M.G. and B.M.), based on an episode extracted from the historical
work of Dimitrie Cantemir which Hugo himself had used,[19] is
distinguished by the lush and studied Eastern technical vocabulary;
as to the epic plot, the principal personage is a sort of Triboulet
from *Le Roi s'amuse,* but a Triboulet who is successful in his revenge.

In this way, the legend which should have grown out of history
gets nearer and nearer to literature. This becomes even more evident
in themes like *Pahod na Sybir* (Convoy to Siberia), which represents
the procession of political deportees—victims of tsarist oppression
on their sinister road to their even more sinister place of exile—
and which is known to have sprung from an engraving in the poet's
study at Mirceşti. As for *Palatul Loredano* (The Loredano Palace),
a romantic legend and amorous Venetian adventure, it would not
be surprising to discover that it grew from yet another engraving
representing Venice, also on the wall of the same study.

The second important group of legends draws on Rumanian
popular mythology and on fairy-tale atmosphere in general. Many
of the poems are nothing but fairy tales. *Răsbunarea lui Statu-
Palmă* (The Vengeance of Statu-Palmă), a beautifully versified
composition, uses mythical figures well known to popular imagination and insists romantically on the love between Făt-Frumos and

Trestiana; certain felicities and verbal harmonies were later to be echoed in Eminescu's verses.

Grui Sînger is perhaps a less popular motif than the poet claims. It is just an adaptation of the Tannhäuser legend to Rumanian outlaw life, in which the gloomy atmosphere—unusual in Alecsandri—recalls certain fantastic creations in the cycle *Doine*. *Legenda rîndunicăi* (The Legend of the Swallow), *Legenda ciocîrliei* (The Legend of the Lark)—the best-told of all—and *Legenda lăcrămioarei* (The Legend of the Lily of the Valley) belong to a cycle of metamorphoses in which the poet takes advantage of the popular fairy tale to invent fantastic happenings. Their only link with tradition seems to be etymological: the author does not start from a popular narrative substratum but imagines such actions as might explain certain popular names.

The other poems in this cycle could as well have been published together with *Pasteluri*. It appears that the poet himself was not quite sure in which categories to classify these compositions. Even *Pahod na Sybir* and *Palatul Loredano* had at first been published in *Convorbiri literare* under the general title of *Pasteluri;* some legends like *Legenda dela Dorna* (The Legend from Dorna), a Wallachian scene in which one is tempted to see a replica of *Puntea* from *Pasteluri,* would have figured more appropriately among the latter, and so would *Toamna ţesătoare* (Autumn the Weaver), which is half-way between a descriptive poem and a metamorphosis. *Noaptea albă* (The White Night) and *Vîntul de la miazăzi* (The South Wind), two continuous and complementary poems, like *Prier şi fata iernii* (April and the Daughter of Winter), are pastels built on personifications, as is also *Gerul* (The Frost); the subjects only approach mythological legends tangentially through these personifications, their real interest being seasonal. The same might be said of *Soare de iarnă* (Winter Sun), an insistent summons to the absent sun, or *Poiana fermecătoare* (The Charming Glade), a romantic meeting between two lovers in springtime in a clearing full of flowers.

In this way, *Legende* are an attempt at a poetical synthesis of his interest in popular poetry, so persistent in Alecsandri's career, with the most recent revelations of contemporary poetry, in the twofold direction indicated by the epyllia of Hugo and by the descriptive poetry of Parnassians. The synthesis is interesting both as a problem and as its solution. They cannot, of course, all reach the same level of excellence, especially since the intentions themselves are not always the same.

Yet the composite character of the collection should not mislead us as to the value of the poems included. We may distinguish in the ensemble two sorts of inspiration. In the epyllia, the poet is obviously not at ease and is wrestling with material that is too much for him. He is at an advantage whenever he is able to replace the heroic trumpet by the fiddle of the popular storyteller. This is not obvious at first reading, for, in virtue of their size, the miniature epics preponderate in the collection; the modest poems in a minor key, such as *Toamna țesătoare* or *Poiana fermecătoare,* are drowned by the overbearing pretensions of *Dumbrava Roşie,* with warlike fanfares and its too motley crowds.

VI Ostaşii Noştri *(Our Soldiers)*

The collection *Ostaşii noştri* is composed of twelve poems published in a volume in 1878. It finds its natural place as a continuation of *Legende,* which it resembles in its Rumanian and warlike subjects, its constant exaltation of patriotic feeling, and its epic methods. These poems grew out of the War for Independence of 1877–78 and are consequently without exception occasional compositions. Their popularity was immediate and immense, but this has nothing to do with their literary merit.

It is likely that Alecsandri's purpose in these improvised verses was not to win fresh literary laurels. Bard of *Deşteptarea României* and of *Hora unirii* and of all the great events of his time as he was, he felt in honor bound to contribute to the fight for independence. Alecsandri thus does his duty as citizen but not as poet. He did it in the sense that he effectively contributed to that bracing of the national morale which is indisputably necessary in war. *Peneş Curcanul* (Peneş the "Turkeycock"), *Hora de la Plevna* (The Plevna Hora), *Hora de la Griviţa* (The Griviţa Hora), *Odă ostaşilor români* (Ode to the Rumanian Soldiers) were then and long afterward on all Rumanian lips. It would consequently be unjust for the critic who believes it his duty to denounce unsparingly all platitudes and padding to examine with a magnifying glass productions whose aim was extraliterary.

VII Varia *(Miscellany)*

The poetic cycle known under this name actually consists of two series of verses which were published in book form at different dates and which also differ in the date of their composition. It comprises a total of fifty pieces. The first thirty-four were issued for the first time in the 1875 edition of *Opere complete* and were written between 1872 and 1875; only a few are earlier than the first of these dates. The second series was published as an appendix to the drama *Fîntîna Blanduziei* in 1884; it comprises sixteen poems written between 1881 and 1883. The title of the collection and the hybrid character of its composition both clearly show that the poet did not aim at a unified ensemble but simply gathered in the first part of the collection all the verses written by him concurrently with *Pasteluri* and *Legende,* which did not fit into either of these two series.

By their very nature, these poems defy examination as a whole. Their inspiration is dictated by the most varied causes. *Lupul şi momiţa* (The Wolf and the Monkey), for example, which is perhaps the oldest of these pieces (1845), is a fable with a political substratum very much like *Zimbrul şi Vulpea* from the cycle *Suvenire* in its intention, and written about the same time. *Scrînciobul* (The Round-about), *Stelele* (The Stars), *Vîntul* (The Wind), *Două suflete* (Two Souls), and *Mărgărinta din Muncel* (Mărgărinta from Muncel), written and published in 1869, belong to the cycle of pastels written in the form of four four-line stanzas which appears to have been that first favored by the poet and later abandoned, and the last three poems had already been published in *Convorbiri literare* under the general title of *Pasteluri.* The reason why they were not included in the cycle of that name may be that they do not show the healthy optimism and idyllic atmosphere which is the dominant note of the true *Pasteluri.*

Soarele, vîntul şi gerul (Sun, Wind and Frost) is from 1875 and was published in the review under the same collective title. It would better fit *Legende* in view of its meteorological character. *Ştefan Vodă şi codrul* (Prince Stephen and The Forest) and *Ştefan Vodă şi Dunărea* (Prince Stephen and the Danube), written in popular verse of seven and eight syllables, respectively, and presented under the name of ballads, might well have been included in *Doine* or *Mărgăritărele.*

Among the other poems of this cycle are to be found a few occasional compositions. Thus the two *Imnuri dedicate memoriei lui Ştefan cel Mare* (Hymns Dedicated to the Memory of Stephen the Great) on the occasion of the great festivities of 1871 in Putna would not have been more out of place among *Legende* than *Odă statuii lui Mihai Viteazul.* The poem *Glas din stele* (Voice from the Stars) (1874) was written on the death of Princess Maria, only daughter of Prince Carol I. Seven or eight poems are album verses, conventional improvisations; they have in common the growing intensity with which Alecsandri laments the charm of vanishing youth.

The most interesting pieces of this cycle are perhaps the romances and the impressions from his travels. In the first genre, the most remarkable is *Bucovina,* both for its popular style and for the nostalgic color enveloping historical facts which are felt by the poet as something living and immediately tangible. *Ieri şi astăzi* (Yesterday and Today) (1871) is a pastel transposed to the key of a romance: the landscape is the poet himself; yesterday is the spring of life; and today its winter decrepit and shivering. *Visul ferice* (The Happy Dream) (1866) takes up again the old lyrical theme of love being only a dream—but a dream to be preferred to reality. Finally, *Omul singuratec* (The Lonely Man) deplores the barren life of the man who has not succeeded in building himself a nest of happiness, this being impossible for one who has not encountered a loving and understanding heart meant for him. Realization of unhappiness and loneliness does not go painfully deep in Alecsandri; yet the very emergence of the theme, obviously spontaneous and subjective, is significant from a poet who has attained the summit of glory and has reached the age when the retrospect becomes more and more nostalgic while contemplation of the future no longer offers the smiling horizon of happiness.

With the inspirations we might call domestic are intertwined a few themes connected with various travels, such as we have noted in earlier series. *Strofe scrise pe un părete* (Stanzas Written on a Wall) (1845) seem to be the oldest composition. It dates back to the period when, ill on the island of Prinkipo in the Marmora Sea, the poet did not know whether he would ever get home again. He was then twenty-four; and the contrast is striking between this stray poem published thirty years after it was written—in which the author aspires to return to his country only in order to round off his unfinished work and then die happy—and the verses mentioned above, in which the work has been finally rounded off but the poet shows neither happiness nor resignation to his approaching end.

In this mosaic of sundry inspirations, each poem belongs to a different episode in his life. *Cîntic sicilian* (Sicilian Song) seems to have been written in 1847 during the spring spent with Elena Negri in Palermo; *Marea Mediterană* (The Mediterranean Sea) and *Tînăra Creolă* (The Young Creole) in 1867, in Nice. The latter is one of the sunny poems in which the poet watches himself living lazily and voluptuously with his beautiful Creole—an existence that is the happier for being reduced to the merely vegetative. Singing, gazing, and laughing are the only actions of which he still feels capable in that bath of sun and languor. By contrast, *Marea Mediterană* is the bitter aftertaste left by such an existence—an involuntary confession which proves that the poet's dissatisfaction and insatiable appetite for new landscapes spring from the fact that he is not looking at landscapes but searching for himself in their mirror.

The second part of the collection *Varia* consists of a few poems written on various occasions—*Zece Mai 1881* (May 10, 1881), *Imnul Coroanei* (Hymn of the Crown), *Odă la statuia lui Ştefan cel Mare, Hora dobrogeană* (Dobrudjan Hora), *Mărgărita*; of two pastels or meteorological legends according to the formula now familiar to us—*In miezul iernii* (In Midwinter), *Zilele Babei;* and of a new series of occasional poems, all composed during the poet's journey through Provence in 1882 when he was fêted by the Félibriens.

VIII Altele *(Other Poems)*

The cycle *Altele* is composed of thirteen poems written in 1881–87 and published in 1896. In the series *Postume* contemporary editors usually add whatever has been published from manuscripts left by the poet or found after his death in long-forgotten reviews; their number varies according to the different editors.[20] Neither of these two cycles contributes much to our knowledge of the poet and his work. They are mainly occasional poems, those from *Altele* mostly connected with his visits to the palace at Sinaia and the esteem which Carmen Sylva and the poet felt for one another.

Only two poems from his last years are worth mentioning, *Fluerul* (The Whistle) (1888) and *Unor critici* (To Some Critics)

(1888). Both have the character of a confession and show the aging poet who, at the end of a most glorious career, still manages to keep the same modest opinions of his poetic art which he had expressed many years before. Both poems attempt to answer the growing disaffection of the new generations, the attacks and the oblivion that have become his lot during the last years of his life. Alecsandri did not lower himself to discuss or defend his own merits or priority, to impose himself on a public which had begun to forget him and to show its ingratitude. He states that he himself is ready and happy to recognize that another poet, Eminescu, is superior to him; he contents himself with the glory of having made this superiority possible.

This distinguished and disinterested attitude was in his lifetime his great merit. Yet it has at the same time proved to be for his work and poetical destiny an enemy much more to be feared than the unjust and perfidious criticisms of his contemporaries. Owing to it, Alecsandri frequented the Muse with assiduity, but not as a lover—passionate at times, vehement and brutal when needs be—but rather as a man of the world, as a gentleman who wields the foil sometimes in sport and at other times as a patriotic duty.

CHAPTER 6

The Comic Plays

THE bulk of Alecsandri's work lies in the theater. In this direction the author is no pioneer. Before him and concomitantly with his dramatic productions, the Rumanian stage had known other attempts of much the same quality. Alecsandri himself mentions the beginnings of the Rumanian theater, of which he had personal knowledge: the rather scholastic plays of Gheorghe Asaki; the society plays of his schoolmate Matei Millo, the comic actor, about the year 1835; and at the beginning of 1840 the joint action of the three friends Mihail Kogălniceanu with his *Orbul fericit* (The Blind Man Happy), Costache Negruzzi with *Spătarul Hațmațuchi* (The Swordbearer H.) and *Bochet tăta și fiu* (Bochet, Father and Son), and Alecsandri himself with the two short comedies now lost that he had adapted from the French, *Farmazonul din Hîrlău)* (The Freemason from Hîrlău) and *Cinovnicul și Modista* (The Official and the Milliner).[1] He also probably knew similar attempts in Wallachia as well.

Nevertheless, of all the dramatic writers of his time Alecsandri is the one who occupied himself with the theater most seriously and consistently, who gave the Rumanian stage the greatest number of successes, and who contributed most to the formation of a Rumanian comic style. His dramatic work spreads over a period of forty years, from 1844 to 1884, and it coincides with the heroic age of the national stage. It may even be said that it not only coincided with it in time but so merged with it that in reality they are one and the same thing.

Alecsandri had a clear consciousness of the importance of his historical role in the development of the theater. When he collected all his dramatic work in he edition of *Opere complete* in 1875, he wrote a preface which is a sort of retrospective program and history of his activity as a dramatic writer and throws much light on his conceptions and intentions.

The preface is presented as a series of letters addressed at different moments to an anonymous friend. In them the author de-

scribes the reasons that from 1840 to 1848 impelled him toward the
theater and the difficulties with which he had to battle to carry out
his literary program. The programmatic character of these confessions
render them particularly interesting. It is obvious at the first reading
that the letters are apocryphal and that Alecsandri wrote them much
later; they probably date from the year 1875 and were written for
the edition he was preparing.[2] It is consequently a program established *a posteriori,* but this does not make it less interesting. On the
contrary, owing to this subterfuge, we are able to judge of the
retrospective image the poet had formed about his own plays.
The date of the image is late, but it offers a personal interpretation
by means of which we may measure, if not his authentic first intentions, at least the historical implications of Alecsandri's plays
as the author understood them. The best method of understanding
him is to follow him, at least at the beginning, along the path he
himself shows us.

On his return from Paris in 1840, the young man—hardly more
than a boy, accustomed to the spirit of freedom of Louis Philippe's
monarchy—could not remain indifferent to the inevitable shock
of resuming contact with the retrograde society and the venal
regime, which were the twin plagues of Moldavian life at that time.
His preface starts deliberately with a satirical picture of this society
and of customs which seemed to call for satire and caricature.

In the preface Alecsandri implies that it was on the advice of
his unknown friend that he staged these criticisms on Moldavian
society. As the unknown friend never existed, it is more than probable that the stimulus came directly from the actual state of things—
from the obligation he felt to furnish the plays needed by a newly
founded theater, with whose fortunes he found himself linked.
Also, experience soon showed him that the theater was the only
efficient means of making direct contact with opinion in an unfree
regime, where the press was practically nonexistent.[3] This last
detail is of special importance in the evolution of the dramatic
formula that was to distinguish Alecsandri as an author. For him,
the theater did not exist only for the pleasure of eyes and ears, but
also as a kind of school and platform. In the author's intentions, if
not in his claims, his plays are what we would today call "committed"; and as such we must judge them.

But Alecsandri was soon to find that he lacked most of the elements needed to plead through the intermediary of actors the cause

of which he had become the advocate. The difficulties he had to surmount were, according to his own enumeration, connected with the unsatisfactory state of the Rumanian language which had not yet become supple enough for his requirements; the poor professional training of actors; and the equally poor education of the public who liked immediate satisfaction and coarse effects and did not respond to the subtle titillation of a more refined art.[4]

When art is still in its infancy, pleads Alecsandri, the author cannot afford the luxury of working merely to satisfy himself. To write for the theater becomes an act of absolute abnegation by which the author curbs his creative imagination and condemns himself to mold his plays unpretentiously within the limitations of the language, the actors, and the audience.[5]

This criticism of the situation is most judicious, as Alecsandri's analyses generally are. It is undeniable that, in a case like this, an author who aspires to win the support of a poorly educated public is obliged to make concessions. But as Alecsandri happens to be a very lucid author—his perpetual failing—it is not amiss to ask ourselves if the above statement, retrospectively conceived, was not an attempt to justify his own weakness rather than an explanation of his struggle.

The author of 1875 who came before the public crowned with an almost European glory and who was unanimously regarded as a king of Rumanian poetry—the title awarded to him by Eminescu in 1870—was displaying to his admirers a particularly bulky collection of plays of doubtful originality, novelty, and profoundity. The author himself may have felt that his dramatic work was not sufficiently polished (as a matter of fact, the following years were to be devoted to this polishing) and that when issued as a whole it did not add up to as much as he might have desired. If so, the state of contemporary society and the underdevelopment of the language, the actors, and the public alike, are merely a fallacious but welcome excuse to cover his own deficiencies: the more so, as they were real facts and in a way gave a satisfying explanation.

Conceivably Alecsandri was convinced that his real dramatic merit was much superior to the results so far obtained. Every poet is convinced that he is capable of more than he has actually done: this is perhaps the prerequisite of poetry. In any case, this is what Alecsandri thought, and this what he stated; for example in a letter of 1883, he maintained that his work would have had quite another

character and value had he written for the public of London or
Paris.[6] We have repeatedly said that Alecsandri was a lucid writer
and a good judge, even when he had to pass judgment on himself:
what was the basis for such a firm and calmly expressed conviction,
in a man whom we have not often seen so sure of himself and of the
value of his creation?

Alecsandri's dramatic invention, his capacity for combining
incidents, for interweaving courses of action, for multiplying effects
and complications of plot, and for drawing characters was very
poor. In his comedies plot is minimal. In fact, when something
actually happens, we may be sure that the author has not invented
anything but was content to reproduce a French plot.[7]

The psychology of his characters is equally summary, and their
depressing superficiality is proof of a great spiritual poverty. One
may invoke the excuse that the people of that time were really as
shallow as that and that the Moldavian public was not educated
to understand a deeper analysis.[8] In fact, this excuse was put forward by the author himself, but he seems to be putting the halter
around his own neck. If, as he claimed, it is true that the public
gets the author it deserves, there is always the answer that the
reverse is just as true. However that may be, the excuse is not satisfactory. An inexperienced public might possibly have been bored by a
more profound analysis of psychology, but certainly not by the
probing in depth and investigation of passions, this being precisely
what interested it most.

The general tone of his comedies is consistently vulgar. This is
clearly deliberate and had the object he repeatedly mentioned: that
of placing himself at the level of a mediocre public and obtaining
immediate comic effects. Yet the excuse is far from being a merit;
and, even if he was right, what we are trying to find in Alecsandri's
comedies is the merit he himself thought so evident as to make him
sure of his vocation as a comic author.

Comic style is not among his assets. In such a case, style does not
make the man. When in *Concina* the author decided to try an experiment and raise the dramatic dialogue to the height of refined
conversation and discussion of ideas, he succeeded beyond all
expectations, even beyond those limitations of the literary language
so often brought forward as an excuse.

His wish, more than once expressed, was to form by his series of
comedies a sort of gallery of types of the period, a dramatic equiva-

lent of Balzac's *Comédie humaine*. This seems to have been a belated justification rather than an incentive to creation. On the other hand, he succeeded in painting a kind of fragmentary fresco; and it may be said that, taken together, the parts form the multiple image of a society caught in its various characteristic aspects. But one feels at the same time that this unity is artificial, and internal contradictions abound. Thus, Moldavian society is represented in terms of dramatic material and social documents that are French. The author pleads for progressive ideas and a wider receptivity to European culture, yet he continually extracts comic effects from the gratuitous and systematic caricature of foreign elements; at the same time, he takes nostalgic and critical attitudes both to the past and to the present; he bases some of his plays on the most immediate contemporary politics and others on an absolute denigration of political activity in general. In spite of all this, Alecsandri's comedy presents a twofold merit that to us seems to compensate for all the above-mentioned failings—not to mention his third merit, the considerable one of having opened the path to a tradition that before him had not existed.

From the historical point of view, Alecsandri's comedies are militant literature and, as we have already said, represent the action of a committed writer. In them as in his poetry, Alecsandri was, in the setting of the heroic age in which he lived and in his political activity, the paragon of citizen writers. The means he used in his fight, the success he enjoyed, the literary value of his art considered as dramatic writing, remain problems of a secondary order. What is important is to remember that his plays were written in accordance with a program of which the primary aim was a number of extra-literary objectives of a political and social nature.

As the theater was for him principally a well-camouflaged platform,[9] the political allusions are not always obvious; historical evolution, besides, has removed us so far from those questions that they are no longer intelligible to us without an effort of erudition. Alecsandri was therefore right to remind his future readers of them from the very beginning. What is certain is that the idea of fighting something, or for something, is to be met with everywhere in Alecsandri's comedies, even in the clumsiest of his one-act plays, which appear to us today particularly childish because they have long outlived their immediate object. Yet Alecsandri, who was a good judge of himself, realized perfectly well that this was the principal aim of his theatrical activity.[10] His comedy was primarily a way of making himself felt, and it is significant that Alecsandri did so at all during the great historical moments which led from the two mutilated and humiliated principalities of 1840 to the kingdom proclaimed in 1881.

This purely historical criterion has nothing whatsoever to do with the success Alecsandri was sure that he would have earned on the stage of London or of Paris. This belief, if it was sincere, could only have rested on the calm knowledge of his gift for comedy, and this he possessed to a supreme degree. It is the gift certain writers and certain actors have of smoothing brows at first contact and usually even before they start to speak. If anyone is doubtful, it is enough for him to reread Alecsandri's prose writings, in which these same qualities sparkle, comic vigor, humor, verve and that joyousness that characterized him all his life and made him lovable as a man and as a poet. The only quality which saves Alecsandri as a dramatic author is this comic vision; his talent as a storyteller enables him to make light of all his awkwardness as a playwright.

In spite of his literary failings and his lack of imagination and invention, his elocution and his gift of story-telling succeed in tilting Thalia's balance in his favour. Thanks to them, the comic author still smiles now and then from the antiquated costumes and dusty decor that were for him a living society, though for us they are less intelligible than the Japanese kimono of Madame Butterfly.

I *Monologues*

In the 1875 edition of complete works the dramatic writings are distributed in four volumes under the following headings:

    I Comic songs (monologues), short plays, operettas.
    II Vaudevilles
    III Comedies
    IV Dramas

As in all publications supervised by the author, this division is not absolutely precise, but it serves to give a general idea of the contents of each volume. For a methodical examination of the published dramatic material, we prefer a different division, in which the comic monologue, being the simplest form of comedy, should come first.

From the year 1850 to 1870, Alecsandri wrote fourteen comic monologues. In each of them he clearly endeavors to present some characteristic type, representative of the society of the time, as a pretext to conjure up a disappearing world or, in other cases, to criticize and satirize customs, individuals, or social classes.

The polemical intention is obvious everywhere. It might be said that the picturesqueness of the chosen personage is nothing but a *trompe l'oeil*, for though it exists for the reader today, for the spectator of that time—for whom Alecsandri was writing—it was only a commonplace.

The real interest presented by the monologue consists in its social criticism. The author was consequently right in saying that he meant to turn the theater into a platform. These pieces, insignificant as they are in length and often in dramatic value, have nonetheless the merit of asking questions, of branding vices, and of eulogizing praiseworthy traditions. We must add that the author's persistence in cultivating this modest dramatic form is partly to be explained by the presence of an outstanding interpreter, his friend Matei Millo: out of fourteen monologues, ten were created by him and the rest by Luchian.

Şoldan viteazul (Şoldan the Brave) (1850) seems to have been the oldest of the pieces which the author entitled "Little Comic Songs"—a term that translates the French *chansonette*. It is an occasional piece, written to glorify the young national army, which certainly needed propaganda and which Alecsandri represented in the person of a recruited peasant. The comic element is almost completely lacking; the interest, slight as it is, centers on the description of the practical shortcomings of military life which are outweighed by the awareness of duty and the national mission.

Herşcu Boccegiul (1851) concerns a Jewish peddlar of that name. His monologue is composed of two distinct parts: one in which the merchant praises his goods in facetious terms and with satirical intent, as when he offers scissors to clip the wings of those who fly too far, tooth powder for liars, and rouge for shameless people. In the second part, he complains about the difficulties of his trade and especially of meetings with robbers, in which—in accordance with the popular image of him—the merchant displays little sign of courage. The author's satire is directed at two objects at the same time: society and the individual foreigner who seeks a place in it. Both are recurrent themes in Alecsandri, but here, of course, they are barely sketched, since the shortness of the monologue does not permit lengthier development. The character of Herşcu was probably familiar and real, for he is mentioned in the monologue of *Ion Păpuşarul.*

After an interruption of more than ten years, Alecsandri returned to the comic monologue with a series of writings in which the intention of forming a gallery of contemporary types emerges more clearly than in the first works here analyzed. Thus in *Surugiul* (The Postillion) (1861), the narrator tells a number of typical anecdotes just for the pleasure of introducing a series of more or less characteristic figures: a German, a Greek who faints when he is offered *mămăligă* (maize mash) to eat, a cowardly Jew, a heartless snob. All these personages are conjured up indirectly by the postillion's tale.

In *Clevetici ultra-demagogul* (Clevetici the Ultra-demagogue), the narrator lays out his program or his profession of faith in view of the coming parliamentary election. With sonorous words and arrogant claims he outbids all comers in patriotism and promises of freedom. The portrait of the ultra-demagogue is probably a caricature of the Liberal politician C. A. Rosetti, whom Alecsandri could not stand; we do not exactly know why, for on his part Rosetti was an admirer of the poet. One can read between the lines that an exaggerated program and bombastic promises are not the gravest charge. The author seems to suggest that the program, far from being an act of faith, is only an opportunist formula; the accusation of careerism is vaguely worded, yet it is the one that would cut deeper. In contrast to the demagogue, *Sandu Napoilă,* subtitled *Ultra-retrogradul* (The Ultra-reactionary) (1862) presents the nobleman who is preoccupied to the exclusion of everything else with maintaining his threatened personal privileges and who seems to sniff the detested smell of revolution in every corner.

Barbu Lăutarul (1863) is certainly the best known of Alecsandri's monologues. It shows a famous Moldavian fiddler who had died not long before, on August 18, 1858: his memory, still fresh in the minds of the spectators, is an excuse for a nostalgic recollection of old customs: investiture of boyars, marriages, serenades, traditional music more beautiful than the fashionable Italian arias. The monologue seems to coincide in intention with *Doine* and *Poesii populare.* Old times are called up with a sigh that is to be interpreted more as regret for vanishing youth than as a eulogy of old customs. Hence the diffuse poetry of the composition which indisputably constitutes the most eloquent and vivid evocation in all this gallery of old pictures.

Ion Păpușarul (1864) uses the same narrative pretext as *Surugiul* to parade a whole series of characteristic figures before the spectators: the Gypsy who has become a citizen with equal rights but who does not seem to have developed sufficiently to fit his new situation, the Jew who has monopolized commerce, the devil sowing the seeds of corruption in all social and state establishments, the plethora of civil servants of all sorts, the Turk and the Russian lying in wait at the frontiers.

In *Cucoana Chirița în voiagiu* (C.C. on her Travels) (1864) this figure whom Alecsandri had made popular in two comedies serves to ridicule the blind admiration of whatever comes from Paris and the snobbishness of a bourgeois who believes that everything with a foreign trade mark is refined or excellent.

Stan Covrigarul (1866?) was included by the author in the section of short plays because it has several actors. But as the others merely cross the stage, the role of Stan is a monologue. Its subject is the craze for patronage and corrupt influence; at the same time, it alludes to certain contemporary events, including the seizure of the monastic estates.

Paraponisitul (The Malcontent) (1866) presents a man always in quest of a job, who believes himself persecuted when he does not succeed in getting a post to which he thinks he is entitled for imaginary services rendered. *Kera Nastasia sau Mania pensiilor* (The Mania for Pensions) (1866?) by its very title indicates its satirical intention. *Gură-Cască om politic* (The Gullible Politician) (1867) presents the alarmist who sees in national and European politics nothing but dark plots and deadly threats,[11] while *Haimana* (Tramp) (1870) is a satire on the new class of civil servants nominated haphazardly, with no special training and no security of tenure.

II *Topical Plays*

In his capacity of purveyor to the national stage, Alecsandri gave the theater a few purely topical plays which he himself placed in the section entitled "Short Plays." They occupy in his dramatic work the same place as the patriotic poems do in his collection of verses, for they spring from the same wish to guide the collective imagination toward certain conclusions of national interest.

Thus, *Păcală și Tîndală* (Păcală and Tîndală) (1856) is an un-dramatic verse dialogue whose topicality resides in a plea in favor of the union at a time when the national problem was uppermost. *Vivandiera* (1858) celebrates the return of the Moldavian army to the south of Bessarabia, a region that had been annexed by the Russians in 1812 and which had recently been returned by the Convention of Paris. *Nobila cerșetoare* (The Noble Beggar) (1871) has the plot of a drawing-room comedy, yet it is in reality an occasional play. The idyl between the two principal personages, sketchily prepared and presented, turns out to be less important than the common enthusiasm that brought them together: Adelina is collecting for defeated France; Ștefan, who had volunteered in the French army, has been wounded during the war that has just ended. Finally, *La Turnu-Măgurele* (At T.-M.) (1877) presents another comedy intrigue between two lovers, but it draws all its interest from the fact that he is an officer wounded during the war of 1877 and she is a society lady who had volunteered as a nurse on the same occasion.

III   Comedies with Songs

Under this generic title are comprised a series of dramatic writings that Alecsandri published under the most varied names: operetta, comic opera, proverb with songs, comedy with songs, national tableau. All of them are vaudevilles characterized by a common feature—the presence of a musical element. In fact, some of these plays were included by the author in the section entitled *Vodeviluri.*

Rămășagul (The Wager) (1845) is a typical vaudeville, most probably adapted from the French. The comic element results from the situation of the husband who deludes himself into believing that he has made a conquest at a masked ball while in reality it is his own wife that he has seduced as well as from the meeting in the dark of two jealous lovers: both situations are very familiar in this kind of show and stem from a prototype that has not yet been identified. The comic style is typical of the first period of Alecsandri's playwriting: the author has not yet started to overdo the debased language spoken by those of foreign origin, and names are neutral without the facetiousness that will become more and more obvious in his later works.

Piatra din casă (Stone in the House) (1847) was written in Italy and is very obviously an adaptation. The "stone in the house" is the marriageable girl whose mother wishes to be rid of her in order to get married again herself. It is therefore an allusion to the difficulty of young girls getting married. But the allusion is not sustained, for the girl has two suitors and could easily marry either of them. Certain details of the plot seem to indicate that the action has been simplified too drastically and without sufficient consideration. The style shows a transition toward the comic style later adopted by Alecsandri, with its exaggerated vulgarity of language when characters are talking to servants, its names which are not yet facetious, and just a beginning of language caricature in the single foreigner, a German.

Nunta țărănească (Peasant Wedding) (1848) is an idyllic picture of relations between peasants and boyars, disturbed only by the indiscreet intrusion of an alien bourgeois that is indifferent both to national interests and to national feelings. The discordant note in this play is the Greek Gaitanis, who is the teacher of the young boyar who has belatedly fallen in love with a peasant girl. The comic style appears crystallized in the form Alecsandri was henceforth to use consistently: names invented for their comic meaning and a debased language, interspersed with many Greek words, in the mouths of foreign characters. The true interest of the comedy lies in its peasant songs and dances and in its new elevation of the peasant to the dignity of the stage as a character in operetta.

The same atmosphere of a village fête is the source of interest in the operetta *Crai nou* (New Moon) (1859), which is very much like the preceding one. *Scara Mîței* (The Cat's Ladder) (1850), is adapted from a French comedy of situation.[12] It is well constructed, as it follows the development of the foreign model, but it is not as well written—except for the verses set to music—which, as in *Crai nou,* are worthy of note.

Chirița în Iași sau două fete și-o neneacă (Chirița at Jassy, or Two Girls and a Mamma) (1850) a three-act comedy, to some extent repeats the theme of *Piatra din casă*: the principal character has no other thought than to find a bridegroom for her two marriageable daughters. In the way the action is conducted as well as in the presentation of the principal character—one that soon became popular—many reminiscences of the French comic theater are to be found.[13] In accordance with his new comic principle, the author chooses names for their comical meaning: Bîrzoi, Pungescu, Bondici. The language is characteristically Wallachian for the Wallachian and full of German expressions for the German, who appears as a secondary character. The figure of Chiriţa, a middle-class woman full of aristocratic pretensions, a dragon of a mother and an old coquette, had a great success, owing partly to Millo, who created the role in female costume. This explains why Alecsandri introduced the same character in *Cucoana Chiriţa în provincie* (Madame Chiriţa in the Provinces) (1852).

With *Cinel-cinel* (Riddle-me-ree) (1858) the author returns to the atmosphere of a village Sunday in a spectacle improvised, like that of 1848, for charity. It is a pretext for folksong and dance, in which the author does not forget to associate characters from both principalities in order to underline, in the year preceding the union, the unity of style and national life. In *Paracliserul sau Florin şi Florica* (The Verger, or Florin and Florica) (1863), an operetta adapted from *Les Marionettes* of Picard (1805), the atmosphere is equally rural but is of a more conventional rusticity.

Also imitated from the French is the comedy *Agachi Flutur* (1863), adapted from *L'Avare en gants jaunes* (The Mizer in Yellow Gloves) of Labiche (1858). In *Millo Director sau Mania posturilor* (Director Millo, or The Craze for Jobs) (1864) imitated from *La Manie des Places* of Scribe, the idea already developed in *Paraponisitul,* in which every citizen dreams of becoming a civil servant, is taken up again. *Harţă răzeşul* (Harţă the Yeoman) (1863) is again an adaptation, although the model has not been identified. The adaptation is not well done, yet this does not hinder the comic effect.[14] Finally, in *Drumul de Fier* (The Railway) (1868) the comic action is only a pretext; the comedy in reality seems to be part of the propaganda undertaken in favor of the railways that were then being laid in Moldavia, and it would not be surprising to find it was made to order. With this exception, all the comedies with songs are mere entertainment and have no moral or critical purpose such as we have noticed in the monologues. In Alecsandri's engaged theater they form a kind of gratuitous interlude.

IV *Comedies*

The first dramatic work of Alecsandri—if we confine ourselves to the writings that have come down to us—is a comedy. *Iorgu dela Sadagura sau Nepotu-i salba dracului* (Iorgu from Sadagura, or A Nephew is a Pest) is also the first success of an original play in Rumanian. Although rather weakly constructed, the comedy is quite distinctive in its conception; this is really remarkable from a beginner in the special circumstances of Alecsandri.

Iorgu is the writer's repressed personality. He is, like Alecsandri, a young man just back from studies abroad; he has returned conceited, an unconditional admirer of all that is foreign, a foreigner himself, disdainful of the environment from which he sprang. This attitude rouses the indignation of his uncle who, being his guardian, drives him out of his house. Iorgu finds his counterpart in Gafiţa, herself an admirer of fashion, blinded by infantile snobbishness. In the end, after a series of romantic adventures, Iorgu realizes that he has taken the wrong road and reforms, thus earning his uncle's forgiveness.

In this way the comedy treated a topical problem, topical not only for the author, but also for the whole Moldavian urban environment, debating the undiscriminating admiration of the younger generation for all that was Western: a natural admiration that was up to a point beneficial yet brought with it a number of ridiculous exaggerations. The sensible attitude of this young writer, who might himself have easily been a Iorgu de la Sadagura, accords not only with Alecsandri's actual views but also with his temperament, which was always restrained by an elegant skepticism, by his sense of proportion and propriety. Yet this proportion is not to be seen in the loose structure and the picturesque exuberance of the comedy. The action abounds in incidents that diversify the interest. The comic style is already full of cheap effects, produced by a multiplicity of droll expressions in various languages by characters who speak French, German, Greek, or Yiddish one after another. All the same, this first attempt is remarkable and superior to many later works. [15]

The comedy *Creditorii* (The Creditors) (1844) is from the same year and depicts the adventurous life of actors who are being dunned for debts. The creditors again belong to various nations: a Frenchman, a German, a Greek, a Jew, an Armenian, a Lipovan. Each of them speaks his peculiar jargon, as unfortunately happens too often in Alecsandri's comedies. The most unexpected and certainly the best part of the comedy is a play within the play. Two actors are rehearsing a scene from a verse tragedy. The poetical diction of this fragment fancifully invented by Alecsandri and introduced *ex abrupto* has great precision and fluidity and is far superior to anything else in plays of that time and to what might have been expected from a poet of twenty-three.

In *Iașii în Carnaval* (Carnival at Jassy) (1845) the plot is drawn from the terrors of a character who, seeing a sinister conspiracy in every development of the carnival and a dangerous rebel behind every mask, communicates his panic to the others in a torrent of misunderstandings, which have no lack of spirit and youthful vivacity. The comedy must be understood above all as an epigrammatic display of ridicule for the fears of Mihail Sturdza's government, a government with no support in public opinion and therefore with an interest in believing, or causing others to believe, in the existence of dark conspiracies. In fact, this tendency was actually displayed on the occasion of the play's first night. The author was called on by the police to stop the show, but he was supported by the public, who insisted that it be continued to the end.[16]

Doi morți vii (Two Dead Men Alive) (1851) is an adaptation from the comedy *L'Homme blasé* by Duvert de Lauzanne (1843), so that it is difficult to comment on Alecsandri's merit. Yet the adaptation has qualities in its own right, for this comedy contains perhaps his best characterizations, not in the comic use of the characters, which depends on the French original, but in their integration into the Rumanian environment that the adapter has imagined for them. The same cannot be said about *Kir Zuliaridis* (1852) a comedy adapted from *Un Tigre de Bengale* by Brisebarre and Marc-Michel (1849).

Rusaliile is a rustic comedy not unlike *Nunta țărănească* and *Cinel-cinel* in atmosphere and style; the only difference being that in the first the ridiculous suitor is not a Greek teacher but a Latinist professor who, in his turn, speaks a language equally corrupt.

Arvinte și Pepelea (Arvinte and Pepelea) (1864) is a curious attempt to dramatize a popular anecdote, or rather two popular sayings combined in a single action, one about "Pepelea's nail," the other about "Arvinte's cassock." It is a short one-act play with few dramatic implications but is relatively well written and is composed of less sophisticated folklore than the author previously used. In the same class is *Sînziana şi Pepelea* (Sînziana and Pepelea), a fairy-tale with its typical protagonists, written in 1880, performed in 1881 and published in *Convorbiri literare* in 1883.

Concina (1865), a little one-act proverb, is more than a success: it is perhaps the very best of all that Alecsandri wrote for the theater. The modesty of its form and intention would not commend it to the hasty spectator. Lina, the daughter of Doctor Leonard, has committed an indiscretion; her friend the elderly Princess persuades the doctor to forgive her, for all of us, she says, have made a mistake at some time or other. She herself, whom the doctor believes to be above suspicion, has something to confess: an old idyll in which, without either of them suspecting it, the doctor himself, many years before, had played the juvenile lead.

The action is that of the slightest of Musset's proverbs. In fact, the author had openly stated his wish to imitate the form of those proverbs, which he knew and claimed to emulate.[17] It follows that the point should not be sought in the development of the plot but in the tone of the conversation between the two principal characters. It is the first example of Rumanian drawing-room comedy and is a real success. The conventional language is elegantly fashionable, distinguished and precise, outstandingly clear and pure, and is worlds away from the vaudeville vulgarity of some of the previous comedies. Nobility of dramatic diction was indeed one of the poet's major preoccupations at that time.[18] He nowhere else wrote so finely for the theater; even the indisputable success of *Fîntîna Blanduziei* is borne in mind.

But this is not the sole interest presented by this little composition. The subject treated in this graceful, sparkling comedy is the conflict between generations, another theme which preoccupied Alecsandri during these years and which was to be amply developed in *Boieri şi ciocoi*. The discussion naturally develops by contradiction: the Doctor sees no good in the younger generation, while the Princess, more indulgent or perhaps more youthful of heart, clearly realizes that praising the past is a kind of nostalgia caused more by one's own memories than by any decline in standards.

The two characters clash with the elegant grace of fencers, but it is obvious that they represent the two opposite aspects of Alecsandri's mind and that the discussion is taking place in his inner self. Although of modest proportions, the dialogue becomes a comedy of ideas; yet these ideas are less interesting than the personal reactions of the author. To the art of the dialogue a second art is thus added—that of a personal confession discreetly camouflaged, such as we have already met in *Pasteluri* and which adds a specific charm to the retrospective judgments of the poet, violent and passionate in his impulses, but indulgent and smiling in practice.

Finally, it must be remembered that this comedy has a third quality—romantic evocation of the irrecoverable past. This is very sensitively done, especially with regard to the enchanted evenings at Castellammare. It is perhaps the only time in his work that Alecsandri shows himself a true and unreserved romantic—the moderate romantic that we already know, in whose fire we always detect the ashes, but who knows how to revive for a moment by a few touches of color the flame of great passions extinguished by time—if not by himself. The localization of the idyl at Castellammare (probably Castellammare di Stabia near Naples) is not fortuitous: it must be the memory of an evening spent there with Elena Negri—a memory transformed into poetry, but still felt. We thus come to the paradox: the romantic poet who could not sing of his happiness and unhappiness in *Lăcrămioare* because both were too fresh and painful sung them in prose twenty years later.

Finally, *Ginerele lui Hagi-Petcu* (Hadji Petcu's Son-in-law), a two-act comedy (1866), transfers the plot of Augier and Sandeau's comedy *Le Gendre de Monsieur Poirier* (1854) to Moldavia. The comedy is, in fact, by Augier, who added Sandeau's name because he took the subject from the latter's novel *Sacs et Parchemins*. This time it is no obscure model, but Augier's comic masterpiece. This is mistakenly considered social comedy, though it is in reality a comedy of family life, as seen by a convinced anti-romantic, a wise and intelligent defender of bourgeois qualities and virtues. That is perhaps why Alecsandri's adaptation is so happy and succeeds in creating an original atmosphere, one which is fundamentally different from that of the French play but which is rendered with much understanding and human sympathy. Also from the French is the comedy *Sfredelul dracului* (1881), adapted from *Un Oiseau de Passage* by Bayard (1849).[19]

V *Ideas and Forms*

Considered separately, Alecsandri's comedies—with a few exceptions such as *Iorgu de la Sadagura, Iaşii în Carnaval* (which may simply be an adaptation) and *Concina*—attain a modest literary level and are more interesting for their value as documents or as adaptations than for their intrinsic merits. Yet considered as a whole, they show a family likeness and represent the inclinations and opinions of their author well enough for us to wonder what ideological assets they brought to the Rumanian stage for half a century.

The ideas expressed or discussed in these works—some of them quite simple and devoid of pretensions as we have seen—are neither many nor profound. In all points they correspond to the image the author himself had shown us when he said that for an untrained public one had to write plays of rather modest literary and ideological standards. In spite of that, a general examination is not devoid of interest, as the ideas in these plays, whatever the author may say, are his own.

The social material which goes into comic plays immediately reveals the author's conception of the social classes of his time. From this point of view, Alecsandri distinguishes and characterizes five classes: the peasants, the nobility, the bourgeoisie, the upstarts, and the aliens.

For the peasants he always had a liking; it is consequently not surprising if in his comedies they sometimes play a major part; even when their part is secondary it is always a model of noble feeling and dignity, representing a tradition—we might almost say a program—of honorable behavior. Comedies like *Nunta ţărănească* and *Cinel-cinel,* if not also *Crai nou,* were written to portray their idyllic life and beautiful local costume. Even when shown in the midst of their agricultural labor, as in *Paracliserul,* their labor is an elegant ballet and a pretext for songs and jokes. It is obvious that in such images there is no trace of realism; indeed, it has often been remarked that Alecsandri's peasant does not resemble the workaday one.[20] His sentimental peasant clad in festive apparel is not a product of direct observation but rather of the rules of comic opera. Consequently, the problem is not to ask, as has often been done, why the author presented the peasants in such blatantly artificial colors but rather why he chose comic opera at all.[21]

The peasant class thus presented is in fact one of the necessary components of the Rumanian social organization as dreamed of by Alecsandri. The type represented is not a literary projection of the present, nor of the past, but of the future, or rather, of his hopes for the future. For him, national life rests on two springs of equal importance: the peasantry and the aristocracy. The latter relies upon the peasant as upon a natural and indispensable ally, knowing the peasant is the source of its power.[22] It is significant that in Alecsandri's plays ill-treatment of peasants is due not to boyars but to aliens *(Nunta ţărănească)* or to a bourgeoisie that has not yet understood its historic role *(Surugiul, Chiriţa în provincie)*.

The boyars, on the contrary, rely upon the peasants and feel all the closer because the intermediate class of *răzeşi* (freeholders) bridges the gap *(Boieri şi ciocoi)*. Praise of *răzeşi* is one of the permanent features of Alecsandri's plays.[23] His social vision is thus reduced to a nation ideally composed of two classes that are dissimilar at their extremities rather than divided by any impassable frontier, and linked to one another by a kind of sacred pact and reciprocal understanding. The vision is obviously utopian and does not correspond to the real state of things because, whatever criticisms might be made of the Rumanian bourgeoisie in the years 1840–70, there is no doubt that this middle class existed.

Alecsandri did not ignore reality, but the middle class according to his point of view was a parasitic excrescence—what we today would call a useless superstructure. The bourgeoisie, understood as belonging to a separate class with its own rights and duties, had no place in his plan for the future. For him, from the point of view of his reality, the national middle class consisted of two currents which were about to flood the land and must be dammed: the *ciocoi* (upstarts) and the aliens. The *ciocoi* were the parvenus who aspired to rise above their natural status in order to usurp the titles and privileges of the nobility; the aliens were the merchants and industrialists who, not identified with the nation's interest, monopolized the country's resources and economy. Two corollaries proceed at once from these definitions: on the one hand, promotion does not exist, and the future society in Alecsandri's conception has no notion of class war; on the other hand, the national interest is not understood as the sum of individual interests or as social and material progress but seems rather to be reduced to the emotional aspect of patriotism.

The upstart type is one of the main problems of Alecsandri's comedies. The problem is not clear in all its aspects: the representation of this personage obscures certain features, at which we can only guess, perhaps not exactly as the author meant them. *Ciocoi* by definition is understood to be a boyar's servant,[24] or sometimes a civil servant,[25] but this term was apparently applied by extension to those persons who rose to some situation of nobility or wealth by other means than inheritance.[26] It is to be supposed that under this term Alecsandri included all social climbers and that his criticisms, particularly severe where *ciocoi* are concerned, were addressed to deserters who believed that passing from one level of society to another was permissible.

For all that, the doctrine of *ciocoism,* as unsystematically expounded by Alecsandri, is a contradiction. On the one hand he deplored the existence of an alien bourgeoisie; and on the other, the formation of a middle class by natural selection from the two existing classes did not appeal to him either. Two conclusions may be drawn: either, as we have already mentioned, a middle class was not from his point of view essential for the social organization of a people, which is rather strange and does not fit very well with Alecsandri's moderate political creed;[27] or Rumanians in general, whether peasant or boyar, had no vocation for a middle class— which ought to have made him more indulgent toward aliens.

The latter do not get any sympathy whatsoever. The favorite butts in his comedies are the Greeks and the Jews, although other alien elements do appear sporadically—Gypsies, Lipovans, Germans, and Frenchmen. The Jews are conspicuous for their cowardice *(Herşcu Boccegiul)* and for their unscrupulous commercial spirit *(Ion Păpuşarul).* It is true that the author seems to make a distinction between the Jew who has just arrived from other countries and the converted Jew,[28] but the distinction, favorable to the latter, does not lead to complete assimilation. People have spoken of Alecsandri's anti-Semitism, and there is no doubt that this anti-Semitism did exist; but it should not be mistaken for an exclusive antipathy toward a particular race. It was the result of a general negative attitude, the writer's distrust and lack of understanding for all foreigners alike when seen as interfering in Rumanian life.

The same dislike, if not more exaggerated still, he felt for the Greeks, whom he depicts as conceited *(Nunta ţărănească, Kir*

Zuliaridi) and as businessmen obsessed with their own interests *(Surugiul, Stan Covrigarul)*. There are, of course, also good Greeks,[29] but it is not mere coincidence that the latter lived in their own country or sacrificed themselves for its good without seeking their fortune elsewhere. Toward those who lived in Rumania, Alecsandri's lack of indulgence and understanding was so great that he himself gloried in the dislike he had succeeded in spreading against them through his comedies.

Such opinions, however strange and out of date even during his own lifetime, were in accordance with the whole of his political and social ideology. It was an ideology fed by egocentric illusions and chiefly by a virulent and exclusive nationalism. One might suppose that his intolerance is to be explained by the fictitious atmosphere of operetta and by its tendency to caricature, and that consequently the author obeyed the laws of the genre, which tends toward extremist attitudes, rather than his own intimate convictions. But Alecsandri's playwriting, according to his own confession, was "committed." Consequently, all the various views there expressed— with a few exceptions of course—must correspond to the writer's political and ideological attitude. As a matter of fact, he never disguised them; in his strictly political attitude we meet with the same exclusively nationalist tendencies that are explainable in the period of his country's formation, but which are no less contradictory to his own education and his reformist bent. The only excuse for him is that the folklore with which he had so many links did not help him to take another path. Folklore in general is not tender toward foreigners, and Rumanian folklore is more harsh than the average by a reflex of self-preservation which Alecsandri was weak enough to echo. This attitude led at the lowest level of literature—anecdote and boulevard comedy—to persistent satire and banter against the resident alien.

The same contradiction is again manifest in Alecsandri's ideas about relations between the generations. We have seen that in *Concina* youth wins its case, but we may say that the credit is due to the Princess and to poetry. Alecsandri is mainly a poet of the nostalgic past, made up of national grandeur; yet his admiration is not without discrimination. In *Stan Covrigarul* this contradiction is very clearly expressed: things were better in the old days because the boyars judged humanely, because people had an easier life, because entertainments played a greater part in social life; but perhaps it is better that the estates of the monasteries have been taken taken over by the state and that upstarts can no longer all become boyars. So, when we reckon it up, it is difficult to establish which are the better times and how far the present means progress.

Doubt makes itself felt almost everywhere. The past seems to have had considerable appeal for the writer,[30] and he believed that life in the old days was more dignified than in his time;[31] yet, on the other hand, his generation possessed qualities as well as faults. The Doctor's daughter in *Concina* (as also Iorgu dela Sadagura) may commit indiscretions, but finally the balance will tip in her favor. The confrontation of generations is more methodical in *Boieri și ciocoi,* where the verdict is given in favor of youth.

Variations and hesitations in his conclusions are to be explained by the fact that to criticism of the generations considered as such is added an even more precise criticism of different sins and faults inherent in two distinct historical epochs. The old may generally be good, yet this does not ensure them against the risk of proving reactionaries like Sandu Napoilă, for whom no equality that would place him on a level with his coachman and cook can make any sense whatever. The young have their exaggerations as well. They are so blinded by their admiration of foreign countries that they no longer like anything at home *(Iorgu de la Sadagura);* they are so Frenchified that they no longer take the pains to learn Rumanian on the pretext that the French teacher does not speak it either *(Chirița în Iași).* Others aspire to reform the language in the direction of an absurd Latinism. "The new language of Bucharest" *(Kera Nastasia),* learned from the famous professor Trifonius Petringelus *(Paraponisitul)*—a name which only half conceals that of the well-known Latinist August Treboniu Laurian—never failed to call forth Alecsandri's aversion. This aversion was to grow especially after prolonged contact with intellectual life in Bucharest and with the Rumanian Academy, where the Latinist fashion was causing havoc.[32] But the poet had already met with those solemn absurdities during his stay in Brașov, the country of Ion Gălușcă *alias* Galuscus, the pedantic professor of *Rusaliile.*

Politics and especially parliamentary politics drew Alecsandri's thunderbolts. Too frequent invocation of "the fatherland" to further personal aims and ambitions *(Gură-Cască, Clevetici),* liberty and progress wrongly understood *(Concina),* an undiscriminating spirit of reform *(Paraponisitul),* and the interested versatility of politicians *(Boieri și ciocoi)* often appear as themes for ridicule and are also met with in his correspondence. Once more the ideas expressed in the comedies coincide with his personal criteria applied to real life. Social criticism is limited to the visible setting of life, which in his view only needed touching up. The writer's reactions were, if not just skin-deep, in any case closely bound up with the society for which he wrote.

The literary means which Alecsandri employed deserve some attention. His most immediate comic effect is obtained by the names he invented for his characters; the names were formed on the basis of words in common use, with obvious satirical intentions. Such names appear sporadically in his earliest plays and become more and more frequent, even invading his serious drama: the majority of names in *Sgîrcitul risipitor* and *Boieri și ciocoi* are formed on the same lines. This was current practice in the contemporary theater;[33] Alecsandri did not innovate, he only followed the fashion. The name is directly connected with the character. A Greek who rents monastic estates, is named Monastiropulos *(Stan Covrigarul);* an artillery officer, Bombeanu *(Doi morți vii).*

An equally shallow humor raising equally automatic laughs is drawn from the corrupt language used by the characters of foreign origin. Such linguistic deformations appear in Alecsandri's writings in a much larger proportion than was usual in contemporary plays and seems to be explained by the poet's tendency to ridicule and minimize all that is foreign. But as a matter of fact, linguistic corruption is sometimes due to provincialisms, as in the Wallachian idioms used by Gură-Cască or by Pungescu, a native of Bucharest *(Chirița în Iași);* or to the exaggerations of the Latinists who distorted the language in order to make it more like Latin.

The most frequent case nevertheless is that of the language spoken by a foreigner who mixes it up with the idioms of his own country. This inclination is already noticeable in the first of the writer's comedies: in *Iorgu de la Sadagura* we meet in the course of one act three characters who sprinkle their broken Rumanian with Jewish, German, and Greek elements and inflections.

The system applied by Alecsandri is quite complex. In the case of a Jew speaking Rumanian, for example, the writer uses pure Rumanian vocabulary but differently pronounced;[34] violent and peculiar derivations, obtained with the help of improper suffixes;[35] Yiddish words,[36] or, exceptionally, whole sentences in this language.[37] The same process is applied to other languages: Greek (*Nunta țărănească, Kir Zuliaridi*),[38] German (*Chirița în Iași, Agachi Flutur*), French (*Chirița în provincie*), Lipovan (*Doi morți vii*).

As a kind of tit for tat, the characters of Rumanian origin in their turn corrupt foreign languages, most of all French. This was fairly well known to Alecsandri's audience, as at Jassy the Rumanian performances alternated with French ones,[39] so that mistakes in the French lines, which abound in some of his plays, were certainly more noticeable to the Moldavian audience of 1850 than they would be to that of today. In *Piatra din casă* one of the characters who knows three or four words of French uses them without rhyme or reason in order to keep up with the conversation. In *Chirița în provincie* where French plays a specially important part, Chirița speaks it in a very peculiar way, using all sorts of Rumanian idioms translated literally, accompanied by the universal apology: *Nous disons comme ça en moldave* (We speak like that in Moldavian).

Among other linguistic means for producing comic effects we find quite frequently misunderstandings of neologisms, the use of which was still unfamiliar to the speaker.[40] Popular expressions of special pungency and comic verve[41] and double entendres[42] are used; less often used is the more complex play on words—surely imitated from French comedy—in sentences wrongly spoken, so that the comic effect results from an adroit reversal of the meaning.[43]

The cheap means to which the author had recourse are the more irritating in that he was in no need of such tricks and dodges. His comic verve is excellent and flows from the best and soundest of sources. Happy phrases abound in his comedies. Some of them have remained in the language;[44] others are surprises indeed,[45] and some were useful lessons for a comedy writer of Caragiale's stature.

Another means of captivating the spectator is the obvious link with familiar realities. As in the Golden Age of Spanish literature, Alecsandri's comedies teem with detailed references to everyday life; for example, there are allusions to the theater in Jassy (*Mama Angheluşa, Ion Păpuşariul*), which was better attended when French vaudeville or German opera were performed than when Rumanian shows were on (*Iorgu de la Sadagura*). In *Rămăşagul* one of the characters has just returned from seeing the play *Iaşii în carnaval*, while in Act III of *Chirița în Iași*, Chirița states that she has seen the comedy *Două fete și-o neneacă,* which is in fact the subtitle of the comedy in question. There are often references to real persons familiar to the Jassy public, as for example, the police chief Urzică *(Herșcu Boccegiul),* the Jewish shopkeeper Herșcu *(Ion Păpușarul),* the fiddler Barbu *(Iorgu de la Sadagura, Boieri și ciocoi),* the robber Grozan *(Boieri și ciocoi).* Favorite books read by the public, among which the sentimental novel predominates, such as *Gonzalvo de Cordoba* by Florian and Mme Cottin's *Malvina,* are also mentioned *(Iorgu de la Sadagura).* There are many of Alecsandri's poems, too, inserted in his comedies.[46]

Finally, as in Balzac's *Comédie humaine,* Alecsandri's comic characters come to life and acquire a personality of their own, and he reverts to them more or less systematically from one comedy to the other. References to characters already familiar are fairly frequent. Mama Anghelușa is mentioned in *Iorgu de la Sadagura.* In this last comedy a Graf von Kleine Schwab appears, who later accompanies Chirița to Vienna *(Chirița în voiagiu);* Clevetici, who appears as an ultrademagogic journalist in *Sgîrcitul risipitor,* has already been mentioned in *Stan Covrigarul;* Agachi Flutur, in the comedy of that name, is Chirița's companion at parties in Paris *(Chirița în voiagiu).* Vornic Hîrzobeanu and Sandu Napoilă appear both in *Sandu Napoilă* and *Boieri și ciocoi.* All these double appearances establish a kind of familiarity between spectators and characters, and this is to be connected with the author's stated desire to present the human comedy of the society of his time.

This comedy does indeed exist and is a living document. Even when he is merely imitating or adapting French texts, Alecsandri knows how to give them new life. The plot may come from elsewhere, but the spectacle deployed before the eyes of the reader is that of Jassy society. Naturally, as in any comedy, it is a society presented under a more or less grotesque aspect. Individual cases are chosen and depicted by the author, not as characteristic of social life, but to suit his comic and satiric purpose; but this happens in every comedy at any period whatever.

What is worth remembering is that these comedies give an impression of life and offer the reader the image of a superficial world in a hurry to enjoy living, a world both attractive and inconsistent, running away from problems. It is the world of Caragiale's characters. The great comic writer was in fact Alecsandri's disciple and learned rom him many comic techniques and borrowed many effects,[47] not to mention the over-all vision of the society he described. Ignoring greater and lesser failings, one can probably pay Alecsandri's comedies no finer compliment than to say that they paved the way for Caragiale's masterpieces and may often bear comparison with them.

CHAPTER 7

Drama

A LECSANDRI came to drama rather late. It is not difficult
to account for this: drama did not suit him temperamentally,
as is obvious not only from his life but also from all attempts he
made in this direction. When about 1860 he started writing serious
plays, his experience of comedy already covered many years and
counted a few resounding successes, so that it is not surprising
to find that in drama too Alecsandri still bears the marks of his
predilection for comedy and his early training in this field. His
technique and style, in spite of the change of subject remain those
of comedy in general.

Cetatea Neamţului (The Citadel of Neamtz) (1856) is not an
original play but a dramatization of a well-known short story by
his old friend Costache Negruzzi. It has nothing of serious drama
about it except its historical subject and the gravity and importance
of the events treated; the dialogue and atmosphere of the village
scenes are not much different from those of his comedies.

His first true drama is *Lipitorile satelor* (1860), an adaptation of
a play by Charles Bataille and A. Rolland, *Un Usurier de Village*
(1859) that Alecsandri had seen performed in Paris not more than
a year before. Imitation is confined to the plot: it is interesting to
note that Alecsandri has introduced a few modifications of detail
in the action, taking into consideration criticisms in the French
press about the development of the action in the original.[1] The
characterization and the village atmosphere are absolutely the
work of the Rumanian writer. The "leeches"—the elements responsible for the social disintegration of the village—are the
innkeeper and the land agent, the first because he impoverishes
the peasants and ruins their health, the second because he completes
that ruin by onerous moneylending and pitiless distraints. In accordance with the principles of social ethics as Alecsandri understood them, these antisocial factors could not have sprung from
the Rumanian village community but were due to alien elements
superfluous to the village economy: the land agent is a Greek and

the innkeeper a Jew. Even the tool used by these corrupt elements to liquidate a peasant whom they hate is not a Rumanian but a Serbian servant. Even in drama where we should have expected a more realistic representation of village life, the peasantry is presented in an optimistic and idyllic way or, as we would say nowadays, accustomed as we are to such one-sided exaggerations, in a "positive" way—as a thoroughly healthy class of society and inaccessible to corruption. This conception, which we have seen constantly expressed in Alecsandri's comedies and which is understandable on the part of a committed writer pleading for a cause, is more difficult to sustain at the pitch of drama. In fact, the theme of the play is precisely the corrupting effect exercised by alien elements upon a social class reputed to be incorruptible, which is an obvious contradiction. But as the poet holds fast to his ideas, we shall have to admit together with him, once and for all, that whatsoever is dishonest and criminal is not Rumanian. "Once and for all" is not to be taken literally, as an exception is still to be found: the upstart Lipicescu in *Boieri și ciocoi.*

The action of the play *Lipitorile satelor* is developed throughout in an unusual dramatic tension that is, in fact, drawn from its French model. But its theatrical technique is that of Alecsandri's previous comedies. Iani, the Greek land agent, is, for example, not very different from the Greek teacher of *Nunta țărănească;* he speaks the same corrupt language and is distinguishable by the same traits of character—vanity, rapacity, and lubricity. In short, his role is comic in all details and tragic in virtue of the whole action in which he participates, his character being specially curious and ambiguous inasmuch as the author does not succeed in exciting the spectators' antipathy.

Sgîrcitul risipitor (The Spendthrift Miser) (1860), a five-act drama, is without doubt another adaptation from the French, the model of which has not yet been identified.[2] Antohi, the miser, intends to bequeath his fortune to an adoptive son but, convinced that the latter does not deserve his affection, decides to leave him nothing, and during the last months of his life turns into a squanderer who has no other aim than to liquidate that large fortune. The plot is not very interesting, and once the miser's last decision is known, the rest of the play develops mechanically. All the same, the action is well handled, but it is to be surmised that this is not due to Alecsandri. The chief interest resides in the presentation of a whole gallery of parasites surrounding the principal characters. Most of them bear symbolic names as in the comedies: Countess Pupăzamberg, the old coquette; Rufinescu, a drone who sells his wife; Clevetici, the journalist; and Tribunescu, the political orator. As we see, drama thrives once again upon the familiar recipe for comedy.

I Boieri şi Ciocoi

Considered as the most important of Alecsandri's comic works and termed by himself a comedy, *Boieri şi ciocoi* (Nobles and Upstarts) (1874) is actually a hybrid and fits better into drama than into comedy. The scene is set in Jassy about the years 1840–46, according to the author—during the period of revolutionary preparation and effervescence.[3]

The action takes place around two distinct poles, quite ingeniously linked together. In Moldavian high society, namely in the house of one of the grand boyars, Vornicul Hîrzobeanu, we watch the rise of a typical *ciocoi,* Lipicescu, a manservant of the nobleman. He becomes a boyar owing to his ingratiating and servile manners, to influence, and to forgery of documents, and also to the careless benevolence of his master, a grand seigneur with no time for such details. Lipicescu even comes to aspire to the hand of his master's daughter Elena. As his efforts to gain her good will have failed, he forges a promissory note that will ruin Hîrzobeanu if she does not consent to this marriage. Happily, the freeholder Arbure discovers that it is a forgery. On the other hand, Elena is in love with Radu, a young intellectual and leader of the reformist party, but of very modest origin.

It can be seen from this summary that the action follows two ascendant careers, that of Lipicescu and that of Radu. Around them are grouped in a logical way the other characters who are unusually numerous, some seconding Lipicescu's efforts or taking a part in plots, others supporting Radu. The sentimental intrigues are manifold and intertwine in a most complicated way. Radu—in love with Elena, who has rejected Lipicescu's proposal with scorn—is encouraged by the Princess; Tarsiţa, who is married but has guilty relations with Hîrzobeanu, makes up to Radu at the beginning, then turns against him and sides with Lipicescu. In addition, there is a long series of episodic actions and secondary parallel interests such as the activities of Radu, liberal and patriotic journalist; the dawn of the revolutionary movement, which at one point almost invades the stage in the form of a popular demonstration; the Jewish problem, discussed in a Council of Ministers who have been bribed by the interested parties; and Arbure's lawsuit with a boyar judged by another boyar.

Such a complex plot might be surprising from a writer like Alecsandri, who is not normally conspicuous for his inventiveness. Here again, not being content with his own resources, he has had recourse to several French models which he has ably combined. The upstart's career and the implied character study were borrowed from *Les Effrontés* by Émile Augier (1862). The idea of an amorous rivalry between a poor but deserving man and an unworthy but opulent financier comes from the comedy *Le fils de Giboyer* (1862) by the same author. In spite of considerable differences in the Council of Ministers, we may find a resemblance to that of *Ruy Blas;* and in the action of the rebellious crowd, an echo of a similar scene in *Marie Tudor* has been recognized, just as Lipicescu's ridiculous declaration of love and its consequences reproduce a characteristic episode from Victor Hugo's *Cromwell*.[4] The twofold polarity of these reminiscences is significant, for they should in principle have been incompatible: Augier is by definition anti-romantic, while the reminiscences from Victor Hugo are most theatrical and far-fetched. Augier is presenting comedy and Hugo drama, or melodrama. Yet Alecsandri has assimilated the raw material thus borrowed ably enough and has succeeded in giving the personages perfectly localized and individualized characterizations.

Their originality is so convincing that in Radu it is not difficult to recognize Alecsandri himself in the years when the action is taking place; he himself underlined this identification by certain details in the play. Elena, as a name if not as a portrait, is a pious remembrance; the Princess who protects her and whose identity is unknown is certainly the person that bears the same name in *Concina;* and the rebellion at Arbureni related in Act IV is the one already related in the poem entitled *Plugul blestemat* (The Accursed Plow).

Beyond the sentimental intrigue and beyond the individual characterizations, one sees that the real subject of the play, as the title itself shows, is the confrontation of social classes. From this point of view it is a late but in a way definitive exposition of Alecsandri's social conceptions, such as we have also seen in his comedies. The enemy, the hateful element of social organization, is the

upstart. Against him is effected a kind of holy alliance of true aristocracy—because there exists a false aristocracy formed of foreigners
and parvenus—with the intellectual middle class and the peasantry.

The title, in fact, is inaccurate. According to the classical definition of the word, the play comprises one *ciocoi* only, Lipicescu:
this word should consequently figure in the title in the singular.
Nonetheless, it is immediately obvious that the author means by upstarts to include some of the boyars. The freeholder Arbure describes
in turn all the boyars that pass through Hîrzobeanu's drawing
room; and from his enumeration as well as from the action itself
one guesses that Neamuş, Vulpe, and even Hîrzobeanu—all boyars
more or less highly placed and more or less authentic aristocrats—
are notwithstanding more or less upstarts. Judging society from
this point of view, we find in Hîrzobeanu's drawing rooms and
in the list of the cast only one true boyar, Stîlpeanu. It would seem
that, following Alecsandri's suggestions, we should understand
by upstarts not a distinctive social class but a subjective and
emotional judgment, which primarily takes into consideration the
human quality of the individuals. In this case, *ciocoism* would not
be a mark of origin but of unworthiness. Radu, whose origin is as
modest as Lipicescu's and is climbing the social ladder more quickly
than he, can never be classed as a vulgar thruster. His rise is that
of merit and is presented as opportune and salutary. It would
consequently appear that drawing ideological conclusions, there
exists in *Boieri şi ciocoi* the idea that it is possible to build up a
middle class on sound national positions. This thesis is new in
Alecsandri's plays and would have deserved more ample development.

The genre to which this play belongs is difficult to define.[5]
Features of comedy as understood by Alecsandri are many and
obvious: in the names, all of them symbolic and intended satirically; in the corrupt language of certain characters, mixed with
Greek by Trufandache and with the Slavonic terminology of law-
courts by Vulpe. Nor are the elements of vaudeville lacking. Yet
the action has a pronounced dramatic character, sometimes even
melodramatic. The tension which reigns all through the action
and conducts it to its logical conclusion has nothing comic; the
conclusion is not the marriage of the two lovers but the fall of Lipicescu, the first being one of the many corollaries of the last, and
obviously this is not a comic theme. What is more, a complex man

of undecided character, neither very good nor very bad, appears for the first and last time in any play of Alecsandri's. This man, Hîrzobeanu, has qualities that render him attractive and sins that constitute a sort of tragic guilt in the Aristotelian sense. All the other characters are entirely good or wholly bad, as is the case in vaudeville sometimes, in "committed" literature always; while Hîrzobeanu's personality possesses indisputable dramatic qualities that make him the sole enigma and, in a sense, the real crux of the action.

II Despot Vodă

Having come late to drama, Alecsandri came still later to idealist historical drama of a romantic type. With the exception already mentioned of *Cetatea Neamțului,* an isolated phenomenon poorly organized from the theatrical point of view, his historical dramas are works of his maturity, not to say of his old age. This delay is odd. National history ought to have interested Alecsandri as dramatic material much earlier: it had done so as epic material for his ballads. If he did not pay it more attention, the cause—or at least one of the causes—should perhaps be sought in the growing alienation of the French stage from romantic drama after 1840, that is to say at the time when Alecsandri had begun to dedicate himself to the theater. Perhaps the more serious problems of composition which it set for the author may have played their part.

When he began to write historical plays in verse, the poet was approaching his sixtieth year. His belated interest (which was soon to become exclusive) in this dramatic formula, new to him but in reality out of date, was awakened both from within and from without. In France romantic drama had been revived after 1870 owing to Victor Hugo's return to Paris and partly also to the success of Henri de Bornier. In his own country the writing of verse plays gained ground some years earlier with the works of Hașdeu and Scurtescu.[6]

Yet for him the really determining factor seems to have been the normal evolution of a dramatic author who had retired from the present after a series of disappointments and spontaneously turned toward the dead past. As often happens with writers who, by force of circumstance, take part in action and come to confront general ideas with their particular application, Alecsandri's idealism had been mortified by the impact of realities. That is why, detesting the contemporary scene, he turned toward history, as he had moved away from social life in the capital to contemplate the placid landscape of Mircești. Only the past, with its hazy and fanciful shape, is susceptible of being idealized.

As the poet himself confessed, the glorious princes and valiant Rumanians of old[7] consoled him for the present and impelled him toward historical national drama—toward *Despot Vodă* (Prince Despot). Despot has moments of grandeur—although this is not the most obvious of his traits—but even if he were grand all the time, he is not a Rumanian and consequently does not represent the heroic national past as Alecsandri understood it. Lăpușneanu is far from being a model of grandeur. Among the surrounding boyars there are two few valiant Rumanians; at most we might mention Tomșa, a secondary character. As to the rest, we must recognize that the author saw in this episode of history a majestic warlike spectacle which his audience fails to see.

In fact Alecsandri did not delude himself, nor did he try to deceive the spectator. Starting from the idea of finding grounds for national pride, he stumbled upon the figure, particularly attractive to him, of an adventurer of the late Renaissance, who placed his Moldavia on an artistic and emotional level with romantic drama in general, with the violent atmosphere of *Hernani, Marie Tudor,* or *Lucrèce Borgia.* This exceptional character, bloody and picturesque, cruel and refined, ambitious and contradictory, excessive in all his reactions, seduced the author and made him forget his first intentions.[8] Yet it it difficult to understand why he did not realize that by proceeding in this manner he was not only going against the program he had set himself but also against his own feelings. By training and inclination, Alecsandri was a post-classic, that is, an anti-romantic; the subject he had chosen in *Despot Vodă,* as he delimited it, was essentially and exaggeratedly romantic, with a romanticism full of contrasts, of violent outlines, of vehement passions and monstrous specimens of humanity. In other words, the writer proposed to express what he hitherto had so carefully avoided, not only in the theater, but also in his most intimate and unreserved poetry.

Alecsandri possessed an exceptional critical sense and tact in his choice and judgment, and such an error on his part is quite surprising. It may have been due to emulation: until that moment he had always been sure of first place on the national stage, and he may have felt that with age that place was slipping away from him. He may also have been influenced by the new esthetic movement with which he had become familiar as an assiduous collaborator with *Junimea;* it may have prompted him to abandon social pleading in order to adopt new dramatic formulas in which art played a major part. However that may be, it was an error that imposed upon him excessive restrictions: this is to be felt in *Despot Vodă,* which is a long series of compromises and concessions.

The action planned by the author should have appeared as a remarkable unity—the history of an exemplary destiny.[9] But it was not carried out with sufficient clarity; the motives and consequences of the actions do not appear logically linked, so that the inevitability of the development is neither evident nor exemplary. Alecsandri was the first to sense that this dramatic edifice was too frail.[10] The dissociated character of the composition is visible in the dramatic action which consists of a series of quite dissimilar episodes insufficiently linked together; in the frequent change of scene, where the transitions are poorly managed; and in the multiple conflict of interests which shift with the entrance of each actor, and are never maintained. Between Ana and Carmina, between Despot and Ciubăr, between Moțoc and Tomșa, the author has, so to say, no marked preferences. Melodramatic technique is not lacking: scenes like Ciubăr's disguise in prison and the death vigil in the castle bear the mark of assiduous imitation of Victor Hugo, the first who had claimed to bring melodrama to the height of poetry. But half a century had elapsed since then. It is again from Hugo that other characteristic traits in the play are taken, from the program of intentions in the letter acting as preface to the mingling of comic with tragic;[11] from the accumulation of exaggerated contrasts to lyrical meditation; from false logic to inconsistencies of character.

To these borrowings should be added reminiscences from other literary sources, as numerous and varied as in *Boieri și ciocoi.* The tests which Despot consents to undergo before coming to the coveted throne, his dangerous journey, his malevolent reception by Lăpușneanu (who is presented as a kind of ogre or *zmeu*), the attempt at murder, the wild horse on which he jumps over the city wall, all seem to show that Alecsandri allowed himself to be guided, either instinctively or consciously, by the structure of popular fairy tales. In each of these episodes Despot is identified with Făt-Frumos of legend and like him comes victorious out of all the dangers and temptations set in his way. It is from traditional literature too (the Rumanian version of G. C. Croce's *Bertoldo*) that he has taken the subterfuge by means of which Despot escapes from prison, leaving Ciubăr in his stead. Linda Raia, the daughter of Boabdil, alluded to by Despot (II, 4) is the heroine of a poem in the *Pasteluri* cycle. Finally, some of the details are borrowed from more or less immediate contemporary affairs: the opportunity of electing a foreign prince, projects of independence, and the problem of the Rumanian mission in the history of eastern Europe are debated in the drama in the same terms in which they were presented to Rumanian consciousness in the second half of last century. So many heterogeneous elements could only result in a hodgepodge.

Alecsandri, a writer skilled in the handling of stage effects and verse yet lacking in creative fancy and inventiveness, does not follow his subject by organizing his writing around a well-thought-out theme: he lets himself be carried away by similarities of situation that by analogy and association of ideas suggest to him unexpected developments, which are superfluous, or even incongruous. Like any classical or post-classical author, he prefers to write in imitation of familiar models.

Thus, the figure of Ciubăr reminds him of Triboulet in *Le Roi s'amuse* of Victor Hugo; the idea of the poison and antidote comes from *Lucrèce Borgia*. When Despot's pursuers arrive at Laski's castle, the latter receives them with a dignity which reminds Alecsandri of the behavior of Ruy Gomez in *Hernani,* and the improvised catafalque again recalls to him *Lucrèce Borgia*. The progress of the action becomes a welcome pretext for literary amplifications and glosses, as if the drama were a mere exercise in composition. There is also a kind of awkwardness in the presentation of the characters, who come onto the stage announced with childish and mechanical scrupulosity, as if the author had no other means of identifying them to the audience.[12]

But the most evident weakness of the drama lies in the duplicity of the principal character: an equally strange phenomenon, when we bear in mind that the author had behind him thirty-five years of dramatic experience and had created so many characters all of one piece, far too exclusively good or bad. This time, Despot is neither good nor bad. His friend Laski characterizes him most appropriately (I, 2) when he says that he has the heart of a hero and a sly intelligence. Actually, Despot has a soul equally compounded of baseness and grandeur, of prudent, unscrupulous scheming and of heroic impulses, of grandiose plans and dishonest means.

Once again, Alecsandri's achievement does not tally with his vision. He had meant to present a virtuous and deserving character crushed by an adverse destiny; and of this he had convinced his friend A. Cantacuzino, who was his first critic and who found in Despot a great resemblance to the ill-fated Don Carlos of Schiller's drama and to Goethe's Egmont, characters similarly shipwrecked, plans and all, by an implacable destiny. But the comparison is not apposite: Despot is not the victim of an unjust doom but of his own sins; and these sins are not tragic guilt in the literary sense, for they are too great to inspire compassion.

It is true that Despot is not without certain qualities; yet the qualities are mainly those he expounds in his speeches and consequently do not count for much. His failings, however, are manifest in all his gestures from beginning to end. No heart-to-heart contact, no flow of sympathy, is established between hero and spectator: the latter does not know until the end whether this character— cunning, tortuous, interested, false in promises and feelings—is worthy of his ideal friendship. His fall therefore not only leaves one cold; it is awaited as a just and normal conclusion. A moment before the end, the victorious Tomşa had prepared an alternative for him, a kind of honorable retirement; but neither of the two possibilities is satisfactory from a dramatic point of view. Despot deserves neither death nor forgiveness: it is the best proof that he is not an interesting character and, if we follow the argument to its end, not a character at all.

The lack of logic in the psychological construction of the principal character is fatal to the solution of the plot. The author himself seems not to know whether he loves his character or hates him. It may be that this indecision, so contrary to Alecsandri's nature, can be explained by the fact that Despot was a Greek and, as such, roused the instinctive repulsion of his literary creator who, at the same time, felt it his duty to love him. It might be the first case of a literary parent suffering from complexes.

All these failings are explained by the unhappy choice of a subject and a hero that do not possess sufficient qualities to interest or to move the poet. It is almost a miracle that the drama did not prove a complete failure. It is no masterpiece, yet it was such a success that all the above criticisms and observations might appear to be malicious or not sufficiently justified if results alone were taken into consideration.

The drama may still be read with some interest, and it bears reading better than some of the overelaborate works of Hugo on which it is modeled. This is because Alecsandri was a dramatist knowledgable in the art of organizing and contriving his effects, so that the hybrid and ill-combined material he has used is presented skillfully and with a sense of the theater that renders it, at worst, bearable. Also, he knew how to handle the declamatory verse that he himself created for heroic plays in Rumanian.

Despot Vodă was written in the winter of 1878–79. Alecsandri had originally conceived it as part of a trilogy that would deal with three historical characters—Joldea, Lăpușneanu and Despot—or rather with Lăpușneanu and his enemies. He must have been first prompted to choose this subject by Negruzzi's short story *Alexandru Lăpușneanu*. At the beginning of the following February he had finished the first three acts of *Despot* and was struggling with the difficulties caused by the imminent approach of the dénouement.[13] The play was finished by April.[14] It was performed for the first time on the stage of the National Theatre in Bucharest on September 30, 1879, and was printed in a separate volume at the beginning of the following year. Critics were not too welcoming. Some of the young ones—especially the future playwright Delavrancea, who was then a literary beginner—pronounced a particularly harsh verdict. These reactions were very painful to Alecsandri, and in his correspondence we find many echoes proving it; but in public he maintained his attitude of reserve.

III   Fîntîna Blanduziei

In *Fîntîna Blanduziei* (The Fountain of Bandusia) Alecsandri abandoned national history and chose a subject from ancient Rome with which he was not familiar. The choice had probably found decisive and immediate support in the recent publication, in *Convorbiri literare* itself, of the translation of an ode of Horace, *Ad Fontem Bandusiae,* by his younger friend Ollănescu-Ascanio.[15] It was also intrinsically justified by the temperamental similarity between the author and the character. More than a similarity, it is a question of an *a posteriori* identification with the character. If Alecsandri was consciously or unconsciously aspiring to express himself, his inborn discretion must have advised him to choose a classical subject, the better to mislead the spectator and remove his ideal image as far as possible in time and space.

For the first time in Alecsandri's serious plays the subject seems to have been entirely of his own invention. There is no question of too complicated a plot: on the contrary, everything is reduced to a linear development, very straightforward and simple, without the episodic temptations which dispersed the interest in his former dramas.

Near the fountain of Bandusia Horace meets Getta, the young slave of a rich freedman, Scaurus. Although a foreigner and a slave, Getta is aware of the great poet's reputation and poems and admires him, which, however, does not prevent her from being in love with Horace's slave, Gallus. Horace obtains Getta from Scaurus in exchange for a poetical improvisation; but it is not as easy for him to obtain her love, for he is old and Getta's love is distinct both from her admiration for the poet and from the obedience she owes him as a slave. Horace comes to understand and admit this eternal and painful truth and resigns himself to bearing his old age with that indulgent and smiling philosophy which characterizes him as a poet.

Alecsandri has once more succeeded in making a self-portrait by means of an impersonation. All the details that make up the moral portrait of the Latin poet are applicable to the Rumanian. In the first place, there are the traits of character Horace claims for himself in his dialogue with his friend Postumus (I, 8): he is still attracted by love as in the past, yet at the same time his critical sense and natural wisdom tell him he is no longer at the age when such temptations are suitable and he now has to fear ridicule. Youth flies faster and further day by day, and the satisfaction expected from poetry does not compensate for the bitterness of finding himself criticized and barked at by all the Zoiluses. Yet he answers all these disappointments with philosophy if not with indifference. Lying on the grass near the fountain which he has celebrated, with a cup of wine in his hand, he still calls for the Muse and puts his faith in her, for she alone knows how to comfort him with illusions and tempting images, holding him far away from the trivial passions that agitate the Roman Senate and from the selfish inhabitants of the capital. This capital may equally well be Rome or Bucharest, and the Senate is immediately understood as the Parliament that so often has been satirized in Alecsandri's comedies.

The poet, shut up in himself and presenting a smiling countenance to the world is thinly disguised. His fiercest and most hostile critic, Zoilus (in reality, the poet Alexandru Macedonski), accuses Horace of not being like himself a soul full of despair, preoccupied and shaken by the great problems of human existence, and so of not being a poet. The poet of Venusia in the play endures the same accusations as those formulated against the boyar of Mircești.

The temperamental resemblance and identity of destiny are completed by the idea of decrepitude to which the poet—Horace or Alecsandri—cannot get accustomed. Old age at first does not even seem to him a real problem, since he continues to feel as young as ever. That is why, when he senses admiration in Getta's attitude, his sole doubt is whether he has conquered as a poet or as a man, and so as a possible lover.

The painful experience of Horace is communicated to us more directly because it is not a common case of senility. With exquisite theatrical understanding, Alecsandri has succeeded in presenting him—and in presenting himself—as worthy of so much human sympathy, so eternally youthful, that his decrepitude is felt as an injustice. Beside him Postumus is a comic version of the poet, for he is equally old and equally in love, but is not saved either by the spark of poetry or by the seed of doubt that, through Horace, concerns us all.

Alecsandri in this drama attained a spontaneity and a degree of sincerity which his other dramatic works do not possess and which, frankly, was no longer to be expected. He rose to it without effort, apparently because he did not laboriously apply himself to constructing and inventing a complex plot but was satisfied to express himself indirectly. Horace, as a self-portrait of Alecsandri, expresses the calm wisdom of the poems *Fluerul* and *Unor critici*, and his reverie, with its tender fancies called up by the fumes of Sabine wine, reproduces the strictly contemplative attitude of *Serile de la Mircești*.

Around Horace teems a motley crowd which seems intended to justify Horace and make us understand why he despises it; Postumus is an impenitent epicurean; Scaurus represents the new aristocracy of capital; and the parasites surrounding Scaurus and led by Zoilus are the same Clevetici of the comedy we know from other plays. This time, however, the poet has been more deeply wounded by the calumnies of his contemporaries. However indifferent he may show himself to be in public, he is more preoccupied with them than they deserve, exaggerating their importance and partially transforming the comedy into literary satire.

Although this subject takes us far from the proud princes and valiant Rumanians of *Despot Vodă,* Alecsandri's intention of throwing a bridge, precarious and fictitious as it might be, between national history and Rome is interesting and significant. This bridge is represented by Getta, a slave of Dacian origin. Her literary purpose, which does not need much comment, is somewhat like that of Britto in Bernard Shaw's *Caesar and Cleopatra.* Equally significant is the fact that the lover chosen by Getta is Gallus, the slave from Gaul—that is, from the France of today. This allegory is a profession of faith which is not surprising from our poet, well known for his consistent Francophile sentiments, but which is curious in a play that claims to portray classical antiquity.

This portrayal, even apart from such details, is not wholly satisfactory. All sorts of anachronisms and historical incongruities have been noted in *Fîntîna Blanduziei:* it is true that there are minor errors, which have been gleefully magnified by malicious criticism. Thus Alecsandri was mistaken in supposing that Horace could have intervened in Ovid's favor, as the latter was exiled sixteen years after the Venusian poet's death, or that a scroll is written with a stylus. These are obvious mistakes that would attract the notice of specialists. What is more irritating for the ordinary reader or spectator, even if he is not familiar with the Latin language, are the wrong metrical stresses, which are sometimes explained by the fact that the author was more accustomed to the Greek than to the Latin stress. [16]

All these blemishes are insignificant and do not have much bearing on the general impression. *Fîntîna Blanduziei* remains the most successful attempt at Rumanian classical drama. It is a strange attempt and perhaps an unconscious one, for, judging by appearances, Alecsandri must have been convinced that he was writing a romantic drama. Nevertheless, the serenity of the conception, the slenderness of the plot, and the moderation of scenic and verbal effects clearly show that romanticism, if it existed, was thoroughly filtered through the author's personality when at last he consented to write as he felt and not as he thought he felt.

Fîntîna Blanduziei was written at Mirceşti between December, 1882 and the beginning of March of the following year. [17] It was read by the author at a session of *Junimea* on March 23, and at another of

the Rumanian Academy on April 10. It was performed in Bucharest
on March 22, 1884, and printed in the course of that same year.

The play was much more warmly received by the public than
Despot Vodă was, and the critics too proved more receptive. The only
person dissatisfied was the author, who thought the action too loose.
After consulting his brother Iancu, he produced a text which was not
accepted in the final edition. At the first performance, Act II had a
sequel which was later cut, probably in order to eliminate an episode
that was largely picturesque. But this cut had drawbacks in the final
text; for example, the fury of Scaurus against Getta does not seem
sufficiently motivated, as the events leading to it have been suppressed. But as the scenes in this episode had a flavor of *opéra-
bouffe*—Scaurus' slaves invading the kitchen and leaving his guests
without food—the author probably felt there was too great a difference of tone between this scene and the serenity of the rest of
the drama.

IV   Ovidiu

Ovidiu (Ovid) meant the poet's return to the past. In spite of the
so-called classic atmosphere and similarity of inspiration with the
former drama, to which it seems a sequel, *Ovidiu* is more like *Despot
Vodă* than it is like *Fîntîna Blanduziei*. Moderation has been replaced
by exaltation; lyrical action has become melodramatic. Although
the beginning promises moderation, the second part of the drama
becomes extremely adventurous and develops into melodrama,
finishing in a quite unreal atmosphere of apotheosis.

Interest for the character of Ovid was already to be seen in the
drama devoted to Horace, as mention has repeatedly been made of
his banishment to Tomis. This is also the central point of the writer's
interest: Tomis belonged to the Rumanian territory of Dobruja
which had been recently recovered in 1878. Ovid therefore belonged
indirectly to national history; at least, like Despot, he achieved a
happy synthesis between national and universal. The sources utilized
by Alecsandri are the Latin poet's works and a succinct biography, on
which he embroidered fanciful interpretations of the relatively few
data known from history.[18]

The drama consists of two distinct parts. In the first, Ovid falls in
love with Julia, niece of the emperor Augustus. She loves him too,
but the poet does not succeed in concealing his love and is denounced
to the emperor, who banishes him to Tomis. In the second part, Ovid

lies dying at Tomis in the presence of Julia and his Roman friends, who have come to look for him and assist him during his last moments. The construction itself shows that Act V is an artificial addition, undramatic and only loosely connected with the rest of the action. This imperfect plot is matched by an insufficiently characterized central figure. Ovid is presented as a poet beloved by women, a sort of Don Juan whose conquests are innumerable and whose lighthearted view of life deserves perhaps the envy of the audience but not its esteem or sympathy. This frivolous character is unexpectedly transformed into a political victim when nothing has marked him out for such a part and when it is too late for us to love him. Nor does his love for Julia bring him any nearer to us, for this beautiful sentiment has not improved him at heart, nor does Julia herself seem very different from the many Lesbias and Neaeras who swarm around the poet, appearing to be more in love with pleasure itself than with the poet who gives it.

The scant sympathy inspired by the poet-lover is the stranger and more unexpected as it is obvious that, making use of the formula already employed in *Fîntîna Blanduziei,* Alecsandri meant to represent himself under the features of Ovid. It is evidently a kind of retrospective dream portrait in which the poet's real age is no longer taken into account. We find in both the same love of women in general, the same Apollinian temperament, the same sensitiveness to sunshine and cold, the same praise for fire as the symbol of social and contemplative life. This Ovid resembles Alecsandri himself in so many points that it is hard to see why we feel so remote from the character. It may have been a mistake to choose this man who loved sun, life, and light for the chief role in the somber drama of an unjust doom; it may be that Alecsandri chose a gloomy subject not at the bidding of his own temperament, to which such themes were repugnant, but of his critics who accused him of knowing only the happy side of life. However that may be, the play is of a melodramatic romanticism that does not suit the Roman toga and buskin, nor the epicurean character of the hero, nor the secret preferences of the author himself.

To this late romanticism, on the other hand, we owe the love dialogue between Ovid and Julia (I, 7), which is the most lively and passionate in all Alecsandri's plays. This late-blooming interest in the direct outburst of passion is characteristic of the new orientation of our hitherto reserved poet. In his prose plays, lyricism was completely lacking, if we agree for a moment to forget *Concina*. It is true that in *Despot Vodă* romantic passion was already finding its way both into Ana's pallid and concentrated role and into the imperious and exclusive feelings of Carmina. All the same, with regard to lyrical declamation, *Ovidiu* remains the most youthful of the poet's plays. Alecsandri seems to discover, just when he has lost it, all the poetry of a love duet. The character of Ovid is thus a final crystallization of Alecsandri seen as he should have been and as he wished to see himself at the hour of recapitulating his life. And it is also a final proof that, unable to sing of his present feelings, Alecsandri always found the right key when he had to recapture them from the past.

In the rest of the composition, borrowings and imitations of foreign models are abundant, as Alecsandri felt helpless without them. The portrait of Augustus owes much to that created by Corneille in *Cinna;* the bully Rutuba is a replica of Saltabadil in *Le Roi s'amuse* by Victor Hugo; Corina, a character from pure melodrama, is the usual embodiment—so frequent in this dramatic genre—of the kindhearted courtesan who is capable of generous self-sacrifice; and in Clevetius it is easy to recognize the eternal Clevetici, the old poet's obsession.

The dramatic structure also uses heterogeneous elements. The popular demonstration, recalling that in *Boieri şi ciocoi,* is copied from a similar scene in *Marie Tudor*. The praise of woman in which the lover admires even her failures is taken from *Le Misanthrope* of Molière.[19] In the amusements of the Roman society around Ovid, there is something from similar pictures in *Agachi Flutur*. The final scene with all the characters improbably gathered at Ovid's bed in Tomis falls directly into spectacular melodrama.

Very often the prosody is extremely irritating: as in the former drama, the poet puts the wrong accent on classical names: Vúlcan, Ibís. The classical atmosphere is obtained by accumulating details from some handbook on antiquity. There is a surprising variety of imprecations which seem to come from Shakespeare and abound in the crowd scenes. Finally, the artificial links established with the national past, the dignified presence of a Dacian messenger who is not intimidated by the all-powerful Augustus, and the prophetic dream of Ovid who forecasts the rise of a new Rome on the banks of the Danube have no connection with the action. *Ovidiu* is a medley

that would have been less surprising had it come immediately after
Despot Vadă.

Finished at Mirceşti on November 29, 1884,[20] the drama was
performed for the first time on March 9, 1885 and is Alecsandri's
last dramatic work.

CHAPTER 8

Prose
I *Style*

PETRARCH lived and died in the illusion that he had made his
name immortal by his Latin poem *Africa* and always considered
his poetical works in the vernacular as a trivial entertainment with no
future. Alecsandri had likewise thought that his mission was poetry
—understood as a religion rather than as a vocation. He wrote
much in prose, yet he does not seem to have attached any importance
to this part of his work, which is contained in one volume out of
eight in the complete edition of 1875.

For the reader of today his prose is the most living and up-to-date
part of his work. We may sometimes come to terms with his poetry;
for his plays we need to make an effort of adaptation. His prose,
on the other hand, requires no appeal to indulgence. From the
point of view of the reader of today, it is attractive, as lively and
clear as running water, and brightened by a discreet humor and a
surprising elegance of style. Alecsandri probably never realized
that, together with his older friend Costache Negruzzi, he was
the true creator of Rumanian literary prose.

With Negruzzi he has many affinities. Both seem to have gone
to the same sources. Their prose is equally direct, immediate in
its effects, simple, and devoid of spectacular pretentions. Not for
nothing did Alecsandri assert his admiration for Voltaire and
Mérimée; all four belong to the same family.

All the same, the author did not immediately attain full possession
and easy control of all his equipment as a writer. On the contrary,
his beginnings as a prose writer had been particularly painful.
As we have already seen, Alecsandri, on his return to Jassy in 1839,
could only write in French. He must even then have possessed his
special talent as a storyteller, and it is probably because he had
been under the spell of his success as a direct narrator that Kogălniceanu urged him to write down some reminiscences and impressions of his journey through Italy, which were no doubt being
related by Alecsandri in drawing rooms. This is the origin of his
first writing in Rumanian prose, *Buchetiera de la Florenţa* (The
Flower Girl of Florence).

But our first problem is to understand how a writer who could narrate his reminiscences with great charm but had never written in Rumanian was to write a story in that language. The solution he found was original and surprising. Not being able to write directly in Rumanian, he first wrote the whole story in French and then set himself to translate it. The original French version has not come down to us; in fact, its existence is purely hypothetical, as neither the author nor his biographers have even mentioned such a thing. But it is obvious that the unnatural turns of phrase come, not from thought mentally formulated in French and directly expressed in Rumanian as often happens with bilingual authors, but from a translation that sticks too closely to the original.[1] There is also the fact that, as the story contains some French verses, the translation of which was an even more complicated and difficult task for a novice, he chose to keep them in the original language until much later.

His solution was perhaps not as strange as it may at first seem. Like all the writers of that time, brought up in Greek or French schools, Alecsandri had from childhood learned to write in a secondary language and to consider his mother tongue as an unspecialized oral vehicle, as an auxiliary instrument, lacking the literary dignity that teaching, tradition, and the existence of models can give.

These models the author had to create for himself. As in poetry, he had had recourse to the example of popular poetry, without which it would be impossible to understand *Doine,* so in the case of prose he could only turn to stylistic procedures in French, a language in which he was fluent and which remained to the end of life his favorite mode of expression in his correspondence and perhaps even in conversation. Well acquainted with Rumanian as he was, gifted with a feeling for the language and with a wealth of vocabulary, which often made him a paragon of pure usage, Alecsandri may nevertheless be caught quite often using Gallicisms which could easily be replaced by more correct Rumanian expressions, and which sometimes led him to plain absurdity[2]—a further proof that his mind always functioned on two linguistic levels at the same time.

The experiment was not an easy one. The initial use of French was an advantage from the point of view of literary composition; but when it came to the equivalent Rumanian expression, there remained a series of problems and difficulties. The missing vocabulary was supplied by a series of empirical innovations in which French words sometimes assume Italian forms (although in fact Alecsandri knew very little Italian) and at other times Greek forms.[3] When the translation or the Rumanization did not seem to him adequate, he preferred to keep the original term intact.[4] His worst difficulty was in grammar and especially in the syntactic links with words of foreign origin. These links have remained to this day difficult or unpleasant to the ear, and it is therefore not astonishing that Alecsandri's solutions, invariably based on respect for the original expression, were not always the happiest, or, in any case, not those that have been retained by the literary language.[5]

What is even more surprising is the fact that this experiment had a most satisfactory result. The quality of Alecsandri's prose even at his first attempt is incontestable. In order to judge of the novelty of this result, it suffices to compare *Buchetiera de la Florenţa* with any official literary text of the years 1840–50, legal texts, press articles—all written in a lumbering and overburdened language, with stuttering syntax and an obvious poverty of resources. On the contrary, Alecsandri's narrative prose is clear and fluid, and one scarcely notices the irritation of a few wrongly constructed neologisms. Like Negruzzi, Alecsandri skipped the whole of the Phanariot eighteenth century, which enriched language and impoverished literature, and rediscovered the narrative style of the great Moldavian chroniclers, fertilizing it with new inflections of thought and more abundant nuances and diversifying it with romantic meditation.

II *Romantic Prose*

As regards its contents, *Buchetiera de la Florenţa* is a kind of autobiographical short story, half romantic fiction and half travel reminiscences and evocation of picturesque background, as was usual in sentimental stories about Italy written by the French. The hero, a young painter, who is supposed to have been the author's fellow student in Paris, has fallen madly in love with an Italian singer whom he has heard in the leading part of *Norma*. This love— which is dangerous because Cecilia, the singer, is very closely supervised by an old and rich protector—develops with an irresistible vehemence to be expected in all idyls on Italian soil.

The dramatic incidents—alternations of exaltation and deep despair, tears and daggers, the image of the Virgin which reproduces the features of the adored woman in a mysterious chapel of the Duomo in Florence, the disguises and, at the end of all these fantastic adventures, the apotheosis of happy and fully requited love—give the youthful story a thrill of bohemian life very similar to other work in this genre. It seems, as a matter of fact, that the adventure was based on reality, the lover being Costache Negri who had studied in Italy and whom Alecsandri had met there in 1839; the flower girl is said to have actually existed, though her adventures have of course been complicated and exaggerated.[6]

But the narrative is not the most interesting part of the story. What remains alive in its presentation is the personal and oblique way in which it is told, the reader being, as it were, taken aside as a confidant. This is done by a secondary person who takes no part in the action itself. The author, indeed, is not the principal character in the narration but a friend who gets accidentally involved, and that only indirectly, in these stormy adventures. But he is the one who relates them, and this artfulness is particularly effective. He talks as Alecsandri must have talked, taking the listener into his confidence, inviting him, questioning him, giving him all kinds of gratuitous reassurances, and making him an accomplice. It is an indirect confession all the same, in the sense that it is a testimony supposed to be direct and subjective and still preserving its warmth, if not its ardor. This subterfuge is the most successful part of the story; at one stroke it causes Rumanian literary prose to attain maturity and find its definitive molds.

Alecsandri had at the same time found his own molds: all his work as a writer of prose is in the same line of narrative—happily so, for it was the best adapted to his way of feeling and storytelling. This writer who refused to confess in his lyrical poetry found in prose a means of indirect confession. With very few exceptions— *Muntele de foc* (The Mountain of Fire) and *Istoria unui galbîn* (The History of a Ducat)—he never did anything but tell about himself, and he never wrote in prose except when he had something to say. In the sketch *Inecarea vaporului Seceni* (The Sinking of the Steamer Széchényi) he actually specified that he wrote his memories of this incident only because he had told the story too often—twenty-seven times, to be precise—and preferred to give all his curious friends the chance of hearing what had happened without repeating it by word of mouth.

Thus Alecsandri's prose has a pronounced autobiographical

character. This in no way contradicts the author's unwillingness to talk about himself, and in each case it is self-evident that he was not recounting his own adventures and actions because they were his own, but was sharing with the reader circumstances which he has witnessed and which have objectively interested him. In his eyes, recollections seemed to draw all their interest from their documentary value: he wrote, for example, because he has been to Africa where his reader has not had the opportunity to go, or because he has talked to Napoleon III and believed these interviews had an indisputable interest for history. But, in reality, it is a question of a literary subterfuge; the author does not succeed in concealing his part in a spectacle in which he is permanently at the front of the stage. And, in fact, not only does he fail to conceal it, he reveals it with visible satisfaction. *Dridri* and *Mărgărita* are what can only be described as confessions of feelings so intimate that the author has been obliged to wear a mask, which he usually does not do when recounting his reminiscences. It is true that the mask he has chosen is transparent, and his camouflage a form of archness.

Even when the author is in principle absent, as for instance in *Istoria unui galbîn*—a story with pretensions to the strictest objectivity, as it claims to be the report of a dialogue overheard—the author discloses himself immediately. Although not wishing to be present, he is lying in wait not far away and cannot help intervening just once as an accidental witness, then again as commentator or judge of the situation. His knowing smile, his discreet wink are omnipresent. Alecsandri was a born storyteller; like huntsmen or fishermen he enjoyed telling about his adventures because a day of his life is summed up in such and such a bag or miraculous catch of fish and because memory glorifies not only personal exploits but also inaction. The game he hunted was a new landscape; the memory, a tune on a flute or bagpipe; the southern sun, his lost childhood; and in all these, perhaps unconsciously, it was himself he found.

Muntele de foc, a narrative written about 1843, was inserted in 1874 as an integral part of his recollections of his journey through Spain and North Africa. It is of the same inspiration as *Buchetiera de la Florenţa* and in fact at the beginning introduces the author in the company of Negri and Nicolae Docan with whom he had traveled in Italy in 1839. As in the preceding story, the author is merely a witness, but here he repeats a tale he has heard. The narration, equally romantic and full of dark passion, refers to much earlier times.

O primblare la munți (A Trip in the Mountains), published in *Propășirea* in 1844 and republished in 1859 with added episodes, contains the description of an excursion through the mountains of Neamtz together with three friends. The purely descriptive parts are treated with affection but without insistence; adventures are more interesting to the author than landscapes. As a matter of fact, the adventures are quite insignificant, which is what gives them their human and literary interest. A scare at the crossing of a rather impetuous river, a visit to a hermitage where there is nothing to eat, and a night at a place where the shepherd plays the bagpipes are the main events of this expedition. That was all that was needed to enable Alecsandri to extol the mountains and mountaineers and to write the hymn of praise to the *doină* which is included in all anthologies. Equally important, however, from the point of view of literary achievement, are his good spirits, healthy humor, universal love, and benevolent curiosity toward all his environment— virtues that remain characteristic of his later prose.[7]

In *Iașii în* 1844 (1845) and in *Balta Albă*, as also in *Un Salon în Iași* (A Jassy Drawing Room) somewhat later (1851), there is a common feature in the search for contrasts between old and new, between luxury and poverty, between progressive attitudes and reactionary claims, which were most characteristic of contempory Moldavian society. Very sharp contrasts were part of the stylistic equipment of all romantics; but Alecsandri made use of them for quite another purpose—to criticize social conditions. In these sketches a satirical attitude is evident; but since this satire has no virulence, it becomes, intentionally or not, a mere stylistic procedure and one of the most efficacious.

Istoria unui galbîn și a unei parale (The History of a Ducat and a Para) (1844), uses a formula that was often applied during the romantic period, and which consists in making a coin speak in order to relate a series of events in which it has taken part.[8] It is a good excuse for introducing varied episodes and following sundry narrative threads that are as unexpected as they are brief. It seems as if the author's interest in these episodes was again social criticism; yet the mild and conciliatory tone of the storyteller avoids all that might have been too sharp. The real interest resides in the varied images of society in his time obtained by vertical sections into the most diverse zones. It may be said that here again, as in his plays, the credit should go to some foreign model, but the local color, which is perfect, is solely Alecsandri's. The work is commendable for its form and for the spontaneity of its dialogue; in it the author found, thirty years before *Concina,* the real tone of drawing-room comedy.

Inecarea vaporului Seceni pe Dunare (The Sinking of the Steamer Széchényi) (1852) tells with his usual humor the shipwreck of the steamer which sailed regularly between Vienna and Galați.

In *Dridri* (1869) Alecsandri recounts his liaison during the year 1848–49 with a young Parisian actress, an idyl celebrated in a poem of the cycle *Suvenire.* The story falls into two distinct parts. The first is a description of the actress' life and a presentation of stage life, half realistic and half romantic, with all its intrigues in the wings and its mysterious love affairs. In the second part, the author, who barely conceals himself under the name of Vali, tells of his own adventures in the period that precedes his encounter with Dridri—that is, during the revolutionary days of 1848. These details form a document of autobiography rather than history, very revealing of the author's youthful and patriotic illusions and of his later disillusionment. It is in the latter state of mind that he recounts his former reactions.

Both parts, then, follow the biographies of the two protagonists until the moment their destinies converge. It is clear that the sketch should have had a third part. In the text of the story *Dridri* as published in *Convorbiri literare* (1869) and republished in *Revista contemporană* (1873), the thread of the tale is interrupted by a gap that leaves out the events between Vali's arrival in Transylvania (April, 1848) and his departure from Paris to Constantinople (summer of 1849). In other words, the author only published the two introductory chapters of the story and two final letters taken from the lovers' correspondence, which summarily show the end of the affair. All that constitutes the actual idyl during Alecsandri's sojourn in Paris is left out.

It is possible that Alecsandri never wrote this part of his autobiographical novel: this may have been because of discretion—which does not seem plausible if we consider the published sections —or perhaps because he himself was, as he used to say of his good friend Millo, "a devotee of the holy Rumanian divinity, Laziness."[9]

Whatever the cause, it is a pity he stopped halfway. If the novel had been completed it would probably have been the best Rumanian novel at the time the fragments were published. The most lucid authors and those who most imagine that they know themselves may be wrong about the nature of their real talent.

The same may be said about *Mărgărita* (1870), which likewise is an autobiographical fragment. It refers to the same period, the years 1852–55, and deals with the poet's love for a certain unidentified Mărgărita who occupied his mind at that time and was the eponymous heroine of *Mărgăritărele*. The poet's love appears to have been returned, but Mărgărita was married, and if we rightly understand a real situation, so carefully concealed that it still remains an enigma in Alecsandri's biography, her husband seems to have been a friend of his. In order to end an embarrassing impasse, the poet decided to leave Jassy. It appears that the separation, equally painful for both, was jointly agreed upon, and later, after the flames of passion had flickered down, this love was transformed into mere friendship. The fragments published by the author, who again hides under the transparent name of Alexis V, follow the principal episodes of the idyl. The narrative is tighter than in *Dridri,* for the unpublished parts were found among Alecsandri's manuscripts. There may be nothing missing of the romantic plot, but what appears to be lacking is care for form and continuity of effort in a more sustained style.

III *Memoirs and Criticisms*

The other prose writings of Alecsandri are memoirs and criticisms. In the first category come the reminiscences collected under the general title of *Călătorie în Africa* (Journey in Africa), sporadically published in 1855, 1868, and 1874. Even so, they are not complete; for they should have contained a final section with the description of his Spanish journey, announced by the author himself but never published and probably never written because of the divinity already invoked. The description is not only excellent; it is perhaps the most successful record of a journey published in Rumanian. It is true that this genre was not very well represented in the literature of that time, and it is equally true that a travelogue is often just a literary pretext. But it is precisely this which make Alecsandri's travelogues interesting: the documentary element is unimportant, while that of adventure and personal experience is always intriguing and sometimes thrilling.

Naturally in *Extract din istoria misiilor mele politice* (Extract from the History of My Political Missions) (1868), where he tells of the diplomatic contacts he established in Paris, London, and Turin on an official mission immediately after the union of 1859, the interest lies mostly in the historical aspect of the document; the more so as, this time, the author is no longer himself, but presents himself to his interlocutors, as he does to his readers, *ès qualité,* in all the dignity of his mission. Yet even in these reports, which are naturally more objective and respectful of truth than the above-mentioned autobiographical fragments, the author's personality shows through.

Alecsandri also wrote a long series of articles published in reviews, chiefly in *Convorbiri literare;* these have not all been collected in a volume. This is an injustice, because his prose is always interesting even when he is defending wrong positions, as for example some of the linguistic attitudes he takes in *Din albumul unui bibliofil* (From the Album of a Bibliophile) (1875) or in *Dicţionar grotesc* (Grotesc Dictionary). His literary criticism deserves a separate volume; the most remarkable articles are those that have served as preface to the collection of *Poesii populare,* an *Introducere la scrierile lui Costache Negruzzi* (Introduction to the Writings of C. N.) (1872), written as a preface to the edition of that writer's works, and his various articles and notes on Bălcescu, Alecu Russo, and Anton Pann.

CHAPTER 9

Conclusion

THE artistic value of Alecsandri's literary work is unequal. And it could not be otherwise in the case of a writer who poured his personality into so many and varied molds, and who at the same time shrank from interpreting himself. This shyness is, as a matter of fact, his greatest merit: for usually one's merits are only the other side of one's most characteristic failings.

In reality, Alecsandri seems to have judged himself wrongly as a poet. He believed himself destined, or perhaps obliged, to become a Tyrtaeus, in an epoch when, it is true, his country needed a Tyrtaeus. He endeavored conscientiously and laboriously to sing of all national subjects: political struggles, social ideas, the thunder of war, solemn national festivities. In short, he acted as Rumania's poet laureate from 1848 to the *Royal Hymn* of 1881. He celebrated all great events with the application of a good rhetorician, of an outstanding pupil; but it is general knowledge that the Muse does not keep appointments on time and does not allow herself to be caught by those who lie in ambush. Alecsandri was treated kindly by her because she found him a particularly faithful lover; she could not have done more for him than she did. His patriotic, heroic, epic poetry is good sense personified. It is we who are not sensible when we try to apply value judgments to his essentially historical undertaking.

This good sense does not suit him except when the poet is really playing his part when, forgetting all about others, he turns to sing of himself. Sometimes he tries to surpass himself—in *Lăcrămioare,* for example—but the lyrical effort to which he forces himself wearies him even more than heroic effort. Yet when he talks about himself with that good sense that is characteristic of him, and especially when he contemplates himself, the poet is supreme. *Pasteluri* contains all his originality as a romantic poet who refuses romanticism. This author who is no poet when he wishes to be one succeeds in becoming a poet as soon as he is content with looking on. His contemplation is not passive but dramatic: as he erred in singing

155

of himself directly and without dissembling, he erred too when he imagined he was seeing objective pictures, for in reality he was dreaming about himself.

On the other hand, the restrained poet—the living negation of the Platonic madness that should inspire every poet—still had moments of enthusiasm. His poetry became sincere when the poet became a peasant. It is a false sincerity—believed in but not achieved—as always happens when poetical impetus is arrested midway. Alecsandri was never a true peasant and never could be. But as he was convinced he could, this belief was his salvation more than once. The greater number of his folk poems are happy syntheses that give the general tone an unexpected dignity, while granting the poet a freedom and precision rarely met with elsewhere.

In his plays, the author is saved, even in his most insignificant productions and his most direct imitations, by his gift as a storyteller. Invention, imagination, ingenuity of plot are totally lacking. On the other hand, the humor in presentation, the scintillation, the remarks made with tongue in cheek are so vivid that they not only make reading his plays a pleasure but they also make them attractive in performance: his way of saying a thing is always more interesting than what he says. Alecsandri occasionally found subjects to his measure, as in *Concina* or *Fîntîna Blanduziei;* but this good fortune was less connected with dramatic skill than with biographic and temperamental coincidences which set him, for the last time, on the path of intimate and unimpassioned confession.

If this gift of raconteur is the mainspring of his plays, it seems to follow that Alecsandri's prose needs no further praise. In fact, it does need it badly because, of all his work it is the part posterity has treated the worst. Placed as he is in the line of the great Moldavian storytellers—between Negruzzi and Creangă—Alecsandri is their equal and shares their fundamental qualities: he has in common with the first a certain apparent dryness that in reality is full of generous and abundant sap; with the second, indulgent humor and a soft spot for people, places, and memories.

Thus from the point of view of artistic value, Alecsandri's work —whatever genre he approached—occupies a place of indisputable importance in Rumanian literature. From the point of view of history, his importance is even greater, for he surpasses his contempories. Alecsandri tried all genres and was successful in all.

If at the end of his life the poet lost the public's loyalty and was too severely criticized by the representatives of the new generation, it was because he figured, *de jure* and *de facto,* as leader in all branches of literature, which could not be popular, especially with younger writers. Although many-sidedness is no merit in itself, from the point of view of cultural history Alecsandri's chief merits are that he raised the status of folk poetry, that he left a vast inheritance to succeeding literary generations, and that he opened up European horizons by his activity and by his example.

Alecsandri was not the first collector of Rumanian folklore; in a sense, he was not a collector at all, being by profession a poet, not a folklorist. But it was precisely this vital collaboration with folklore (to which after him only Eminescu was drawn) that gave folklore its literary dignity, a dignity which perhaps it has nowadays only in Rumanian literature. For other nations popular poetry has been used as document and reference. For Alecsandri and for those who have followed in his steps, national poetry is Rumanian space, with all its cosmic implications, mystical and historical—the sole chance of survival for the nation.

Alecsandri is at the same time and in great measure a creator of this popular poetry. *Miorița,* for example, is the *Miorița* of Alecsandri; and the same could be said of all the ballads to which he set his hand. He put something of himself into all of them—his classical vision, the clarity of his opinions, his cosmic tranquillity, the regularity of his utterance. From the limping text of ballad singers, rusty relics of a beauty almost lost, Alecsandri refashioned a precious metal, whose pure sound has never since been impaired.

Alecsandri was a valuable example for the literature of succeeding generations. Eminescu has assessed with precision and generosity the character and extent of his genius; but it was not the context in which to say how much he, and with him all the poets of his time, owed to Alecsandri. All have recognized that Rumanian poetry begins with *Doine* and flows from it, just as *Iorgu de la Sadagura* brought the Rumanian theater into existence. The paths he opened have been trod again and again by many writers—we might even say by all. Eminescu admired and studied him, and echoes of Alecsandri's muse often resound with a new and inimitable quality of tone in his verses. It was by contact with Alecsandri that Caragiale has developed his comic verve both in his plays and in *Momente.* The travel descriptions of Hogaș are fed on the memory of Alecsandri's. From Sadoveanu's historical novels to the now forgotten

ones of Becescu-Silvan, the heroic atmosphere of *Legende* domi-
nates epic inspiration founded on Rumanian themes.

Finally, it seems a paradox that Alecsandri, a devotee at the
patriotic altar of his country and of popular and traditional literature, should have been the writer who most made them known in
the milieu of world literature. The paradox is only apparent since
world literature is only the sum of local and national efforts: it may
be said that the more firmly a literature is anchored in the present
and in a geography that is precisely defined, the more chances it
has of becoming universal. Certainly Alecsandri's poetry was the
first to pass the language barrier and, as his poetry largely merges
into folk poetry, this breakthrough far transcends the personal
destiny of a poet, however important he may be.

This is the poet who judged himself so severely: "I have never
had many illusions about my productions"[1] and again "I have
more heart than mind."[2] His only failing was not to be sufficiently
sincere with himself and allow that heart to speak more freely,
less tightly curbed by his mind. But even so, few have achieved
as much as he has done, and none more.

Notes and References

(In references given below, place of publication, unless otherwise stated, is Bucharest.)

Chapter One

1. In Paris, when he enrolled for the baccalaureate, Alecsandri stated that he was born at Bacău on June 14, 1819. In general, experts prefer the date 1821. V. Alecsandri, *Poeziile,* ed. E. Rădulescu-Pogoneanu (Craiova, 1940), vol. I, pp. 6–7, adopts the date 1819, arguing that: (a) Sixteen was at that time the minimum age in France for admission to the baccalaureate (but perhaps for that very reason Alecsandri, if born in 1821, made a false statement); (b) The poet's assertion that he was christened by his mother's brother, Mihail Cozoni, who died at Drăgăşani on June 7, 1821; (c) The title of *comis* granted to the poet on July 20, 1833, when the code of Caragea, still in force, forbade ennoblement during minority. The second argument is the most cogent.

2. This emerges from the sketch *Înecarea vaporului Seceni.* Cf. V. Alecsandri, *Proză,* ed. A. Marcu, Craiova, p. 92. From a letter to Ollănescu-Ascanio in 1889 (V. Alecsandri, *Corespondenţă,* ed. M. Anineanu, Bucharest, 1960, p. 266), it is clear that he was able forty years later to remember and reproduce exactly a Greek sentence heard in Athens.

3. Most of the allusions are typical schoolboy humor. Cf. in V. Alecsandri, *Corespondenţă,* ed. M. Anineanu, 1960, p. 68.

4. For Alecsandri's first poems in French, cf. Ch. Drouhet, *Vasile Alecsandri şi scriitorii francezi,* Bucharest, 1924, p. 12–13.

5. It is perhaps significant that in *Iorgu de la Sadagura* the Frenchified student who no longer feels at home when he comes back to his own country is not greeted by parents, but by an uncle.

6. Alecsandri nevertheless continued to write his correspondence in French. This part of his work is by no means the least interesting. It was in French too that he wrote the journal of his travels in Italy with Elena Negri, and somewhat later the comedy *Les Bonnets de la Comtesse;* even in the last days of his life he was thinking of a French adaptation of his drama *Ovidiu,* on which he actually started work.

7. Quoted by G.C. Nicolescu, *Viaţa lui Vasile Alecsandri,* Bucharest, 1965, pp. 75–76.

8. Cf. Ion Ghica, *Scrisori către Vasile Alecsandri,* 1887, p. 253.

9. Possibly the poet's many excursions in the summer of 1840 are to be explained by such secret political contacts.

Chapter Two

1. Immediately after his return he wrote from Jassy to Elena Negri's sister, Zulnia: "I cannot boast that I have returned to Moldavia stronger than I set out—on the contrary—but it is all the same to me." V. Alecsandri, *Corespondență,* ed. M. Anineanu, p. 233.

2. The text of Bălcescu's recommendations is reproduced in G. C. Nicolescu, *Viața lui Vasile Alecsandri,* p. 154.

3. The text is reproduced in G. C. Nicolescu, *Viața lui Vasile Alecsandri,* p. 192.

4. The poem was published in the same year in the Brașov review *Foaie pentru minte* and is included in the cycle *Mărgăritărele* as No. 1. It was published on handbills, once with this title and a second time with the title *Deșteptarea României.* It is generally considered that the poem was written and printed at Jassy in March, 1848 (G. Bogdan-Duică, *Vasile Alecsandri,* p. 25; Vasile Alecsandri, *Poeziile,* ed. E. Rădulescu-Pogoneanu [Craiova, 1940], I, 105; G.C. Nicolescu, *Viața lui Vasile Alecsandri,* p. 171); and in fact this is stated by Alecsandri himself in an autobiographical memoir written for A. Ubicini (V. Alecsandri, *Scrisori* [1964], p. 150). It seems to us more probable that the poet antedates it, whether intentionally or not. If he had really circulated on handbills in 1848 such a clear instigation to armed rebellion, it is inconceivable that the Moldavian government would not have taken measures against him.

5. G. C. Nicolescu, *Viața lui Vasile Alecsandri,* pp. 217–18, asserts that the poem was written in Paris and falsely dated.

6. Nevertheless there are antecedents, especially in the literary propaganda undertaken in connection with the Greek war of independence and known as the Philhellenic movement, and in the campaign in favor of Poland. The efforts of the Rumanian revolutionary committee are, if not the first, among the first attempts at *organized* literary propaganda.

7. Cf. in a letter addressed to Ion Ghica on December 1, 1849 (V. Alecsandri, *Corespondență,* ed. M. Anineanu, p. 58): "Mon épouse, qui fait ma gloire et mon bonheur." N. Petrașcu, *V. Alecsandri* (1894), p. 19, asserts that he knew from the poet that he had thought of marrying Dridri.

8. Cf. the letter to Ion Ghica (G. C. Nicolescu, *Viața lui Vasile Alecsandri,* p. 225–26): "God is great and Justice will end by being his prophet . . . Then we shall become her most fanatical secretaries and will renew the work which has scarcely been begun."

9. Iancu Alecsandri had reached the rank of lieutenant-colonel in the Moldavian army.

10. Maria Cantacuzino, a friend of Hermiona Asaki, Quinet's wife, was later the wife of Puvis de Chavannes and his model for Saint

Geneviève in the Pantheon frescoes. It is thought (G. Bogdan-Duică, *V. Alecsandri,* p. 32; V. Alecsandri, *Poeziile,* ed. E. Rădulescu-Pogoneanu [Craiova, 1940], I, 145–49), but without sufficient grounds, that Alecsandri was in love with her and sang of her under the name of Mărgărita.

11. The printing of this volume of Rumanian verse in Paris cannot, however, be explained, it seems, by fussiness about its looks; perhaps it was a way of protesting against the obstacles placed in the way of literature by the Moldavian censorship and against the suppression of *România literară.*

12. For this person, cf. E. D. Tappe, "Alecsandri and the English" in *Revue des Études Roumaines,* II (1954), 153–68.

13. Cf. Al. Busuioceanu, "Una historia romántica: don Juan Valera y Lucia Paladi" in *Revue des Études Roumaines,* I (1953), 27–43.

14. Cf. N. N. Condeescu, "Relațiile lui Prosper Mérimée cu Vasile Alecsandri" in *Revista de filologie romanică și germanică,* V (1961), 225–39.

15. Catinca Rolla in any case died soon after this on December 15, 1857. For her, cf. V. Alecsandri, *Poeziile,* ed. E. Rădulescu-Pogoneanu, I, 14–25.

16. V. Alecsandri, *Vasile Porojan* in V. Alecsandri, *Proză,* ed. A. Marcu (Craiova, 1930), p. 114. The author adds: "This voluntary return to slavery made me think a great deal about how to free people who are slaves from birth and I am convinced that, inhuman as it is to deprive a man of liberty, it is just as irresponsible to free a slave suddenly without preparing him for the happiness which awaits him."

17. Édouard Grenier (1819–1901), writer and poet, had been introduced to Alecsandri by Ubicini and Mérimée, and by Alecsandri to Prince Grigore Ghica, whose secretary he was in 1855–57.

18. Letter to Ion Ghica from Mircești, June 30, 1860; cf. V. Alecsandri, *Poeziile,* ed. E. Radulescu-Pogoneanu, I, p. 201.

Chapter Three

1. Paulina Lukasiewicz was born on January 1, 1841. She was therefore sixteen years old at the time of the idyl.

2. Cf. V. Alecsandri, *Poeziile,* ed. E. Rădulescu-Pogoneanu, I, 217.

3. He himself invoked this oath later on to his daughter; but it may have been a mere excuse.

4. V. Alecsandri, *Scrisori, Insemnări,* ed. M. Anineanu, (Bucharest, 1964), p. 117.

5. The Italian government had put at the disposal of the Hungarian refugees 50,000 rifles to maintain armed rebellion against Austria.

6. The agency had been created by the influence of Vasile Alecsandri himself, as minister of foreign affairs, on September 7, 1860. Cf. Cornelia C. Bodea, "Din acțiunea de pregătire a Agenției diplomatice de la Paris" in *Studii și cercetări științifice-istorice* (Academia R.P.R., Filiala Iași), 1960, 6, pp. 121–48.

7. V. Alecsandri, *Corespondență,* ed. M. Anineanu, pp. 192–93: "When I consult my conscience and ask it whether I have truly served my country for twenty years, my conscience unhesitatingly answers 'Yes!' and consequently gives me full right to do something at last for myself, after having done so much for others. This does not mean that I consider my duties to Rumania completed."

8. She had two daughters by him; but this marriage was soon dissolved. Her second marriage, in 1883, was to George Bogdan. Intelligent, refined, and cheerful by nature, Maria resembled her father physically. No doubt she also resembled him in temperament, for she seems to have suffered from the same instability of character.

9. V. Alecsandri, *Lettres inédites à Éd. Grenier* (Paris, 1901), p. 59.

10. Al. Cioranescu, 'La Roumanie dans la nouvelle litterature provençale' in *Comparative Literature,* II (1950), 107–25.

11. V. Alecsandri, *Scrisori, Însemnări,* ed. M. Anineanu, p. 59.

12. Z. N. Popp, *Catalogul corespondenței lui Mihail Kogălniceanu* (1959), pp. 359–61. For other rumors of appointments abroad, in December, 1882, cf. V. Alecsandri, *Scrisori, Însemnări,* ed. M. Anineanu, pp. 53–54.

13. Paulina Alecsandri died on February 19, 1921. In 1914 she had presented the house at Mircești to the Rumanian Academy, which built the poet's mausoleum, inaugurated on June 2, 1928. The house was turned into a museum and suffered in the course of World War II.

Chapter Four

1. Cf. V. Alecsandri, *Scrisori, Însemnări,* ed. M. Anineanu, p. 146.

2. Quoted by Alfred Bougeault, *Histoires des littératures étrangeres,* vol. II (Paris, 1876), p. 544.

3. Cf. Gh. Vrabie, in Alecsandri, *Poezii populare* (Bucharest, 1965), vol. I, pp. 32–33.

4. Cf. the note in the journal. V. Alecsandri, *Scrisori, Însemnări,* ed. M. Anineanu, p. 180.

5. Alecsandri, *Poezii populare* (1965), vol. II, p. 347.

6. As regards the political effectiveness of poetry, Alecsandri must surely have remembered the stir caused by Fauriel's publication of Greek poems and the part played by that collection in the forming of Philhellenist opinion in western Europe.

7. The printing, undertaken at the expense of the Elena Doamna Home at Bucharest, to which Alecsandri had given the copyright, was supervised by Dr. Carol Davila. The poet regretted that a complete collection had not been published, which implies that he had other texts which remained unpublished, *Catalogul corespondenței lui Vasile Alecsandri,* ed. M. Anineanu, 1957, p. 129, no. 507. This is confirmed by other sources.

8. Letter from Paris, October 25, 1851, in *Catalogul corespondenței lui Vasile Alecsandri,* ed. M. Anineanu, 1957, p. 71, no. 320.

9. V. Alecsandri, *Scrisori, Însemnări,* ed. M. Anineanu, p. 147.

10. Alecsandri claims in a note (*Poezii populare,* vol. II, p. 24) that it is a "legend," allegorically representing the discovery of mineral waters at Mehadia by Hercules. In his autobiographical letter addressed to Ubicini, he states that in 1847 he traveled to Mehadia "où je découvris la ballade d'Hercule" (V. Alecsandri, *Scrisori, Însemnări,* ed. M. Anineanu [1964], p. 150.) But the "popular" memory of Hercules is objectively impossible. The poem is a cento of authentic popular verses joined together with a skill which leads us to suppose that the author is Alecsandri himself. But he has made two mistakes which give him away—apart from the choice of subject. He uses the Moldavian word *mezină* in the sense of "middle," which it never has in Rumanian; only an educated author could have made the connection between this word of Slavonic origin and the Latin *medianus.* Similarly he used the word *neră,* which does not exist in Rumanian, in the sense of "water"; no doubt he was borrowing the Greek *nerò* to give the ballad an antique flavor without realizing that the word is peculiar to Modern Greek.

11. Alecsandri, *Pasteluri,* p. viii, note.

12. Best known are the publications of M. Schwarzfeld (see Selected Bibliography).

13. Comparison of the strictly stylistic corrections introduced in successive editions goes beyond the scope of this book, but can be made with fair ease by consulting the variants printed in *Poezii populare* (1965), vol. II.

14. Alecsandri was not actually the first Rumanian collector. Not to mention certain earlier manuscript collections, Asachi claimed the title for himself, but he published nothing in this field. The collection of Atanasie Marienescu was printed in 1859, between the two editions of Alecsandri's.

15. Some of Ubicini's translations, probably done with the help of Alecsandri, had been first published in *Revue de l'Orient,* XV (1854), 302–20; I (1855), 385–91; II (1855), 227–45.

16. H. Tostard, "Bogdan, légende bulgare" in *Revue anglo-francaise,* V (1877), 286–87, is a curious plagiarism of the ballad of that name in Alecsandri's collection, but disguised in Bulgarian dress. Cf. also Auguste Picq and Ph. Breban, "La légende de Curtea de Argis" in *Revue de France,* V (1879), 329–52 and 485–502.

17. V. Alecsandri, *Scrisori, Insemnări,* ed. M. Anineanu, p. 147.

Chapter Five

1. They appeared in the review *Spicuitorul moldo-român (Le Glaneur moldo-valaque),* which was published at Jassy in Rumanian and French. The poems *Le Cosaque, La jeune Fille,* and *A.M. de Lamartine* were published in 1841. The Rumanian translations accompanying them were by Ion Poni, D. Gusti and Gh. Asaki, respectively. On the other hand, MS

French 178 in the Rumanian Academy at Bucharest contains twenty-four French poems by Alecsandri, which should be published.

2. V. Alecsandri, *Proză,* ed. A. Marcu, pp. 140–41. At a time when education was conducted exclusively in Greek, this is neither a unique case nor a surprising one. Heliade Rădulescu has related very amusingly (*'Cum am învăţat româneşte')* how he learned Rumanian by stealth while playing truant from school; and almost all the great writers of the 1840 generation wrote French more fluently than they did Rumanian.

3. V. Alecsandri, *Poesii populare,* vol. I, p. 64.

4. The poems *Crai-nou, Groza,* and *Cinel-cinel.* The poem *Altarul Mănăstirii Putna* is written in lines of sixteen syllables; but this is merely a typographical arrangement, inasmuch as each half line could be considered an eight-syllable line, and so a popular type.

5. V. Alecsandri, *Corespondenţă,* ed. M. Anineanu, p. 68.

6. Notices of the French translation in Jules Michelet, *Légendes démocratiques du Nord;* Xavier Marmier, *Voyages et Littérature* (Paris, 1888), pp. 39–96; A. Grun, *"Les Doinas"* in *Revue de l'Orient,* XV (1854); G. Vegezzi-Ruscalla in *Lo Spettatore* (1855), No. 35.

7. Cf. Al. Cioranescu, "Scriitorii români şi Italia" in *Roma* (Bucharest, 1932–33); B. Munteanu, "Moments vénitiens dans la littérature roumaine" in *Convivium,* IV (1946), 197–212.

8. Cf. the letter addressed to Negri in V. Alecsandri, *Corespondenţă,* ed. M. Anineanu (1960), p. 157. It is thought (cf. Alecsandri, *Opere,* vol. I, pp. 234–35) that this consultation was due to literary scruples and that Negri was in this case the poet's critical adviser; but the context clearly shows that Alecsandri's attitude of reserve concerned the moral and social timeliness of publication.

9. This poem, or at least the first two lines, served later as words for a religious hymn which is still sung in Holy Week.

10. Cf. V. Alecsandri, *Poeziile,* ed. E. Rădulescu-Pogoneanu, vol. II, p. 3.

11. V. Alecsandri, *Opere,* vol. I, pp. 445–46.

12. Vaillant, *La Romanie* (Paris, 1844), vol. I.

13. Cf. Charles Drouhet, "Ronsard şi România" in *Convorbiri literare* (1924), pp. 521–24, 846–50: N. Iorga, "Ronsard et la Roumanie" in *Muse française* (1924), pp. 231–36.

14. Alecsandri's was not a one-track road; he wrote the *Doine* at the same time he wrote the poems in *Lăcrimioare* and *Suvenire.* The division into cycles was conceived *a posteriori,*

15. According to Ch. Drouhet, *Vasile Alecsandri şi scriitorii francezi,* p. 43, the idea for this poem comes from Victor Hugo's *L'Église;* but cf. Tasso, *Gerusalemme liberata,* XVI, 12–17. It is certain that he was reading Tasso at that time, because he remembered him in *Legende.*

16. Cf. Ch. Drouhet, *Vasile Alecsandri și scriitorii francezi,* p. 50.

17. In reality it was not lacking, because Budai-Deleanu's *Țiganiada* is much earlier; but by classic canons it was a comic-heroic poem, not an epic.

18. Cf. Ch. Drouhet, *Vasile Alecsandri și scriitorii francezi,* p. 50.

19. Perhaps Alecsandri knew Alphonse Royer's article "Becri-Mustapha" in *Salon littéraire* (October 6, 1842).

20. In Adamescu's edition the section *Postume* includes thirty-seven poems.

Chapter Six

1. Alecsandri, *Teatru,* vol. I, "Prefață."

2. E.g., in the letter dated March, 1848 (*Teatru,* vol. I, p. xvii), he speaks of a revolution which will shortly break out: an idea which could neither have occurred to him nor have been written down at that date.

3. Alecsandri, *Teatru,* vol. I, p. ix: "I planned to make the theater an instrument for the castigation of the bad habits and absurdities of our society." Cf. in his letter to Ion Ghica, October 3, 1850 (V. Alecsandri, *Corespondență,* ed. M. Anineanu, p. 61): "C'est encore le seule tribune qui nous reste et j'en profite pour nourrir certains sentiments qu'on cherche à étouffer."

4. *Teatru,* vol. I, p. x. The same difficulties are mentioned in a letter of 1852 to Ion Ghica (V. Alecsandri, *Corespondență,* ed. M. Anineanu, [1960], p. 65) and in another of 1865 to A. Hurmuzachi (V. Alecsandri, *Corespondență,* ed. M. Anineanu, [1960], p. 135).

5. *Teatru,* vol. I, p. xi.

6. Letter to Ion Ghica in V. Alecsandri, *Corespondență,* ed. M. Anineanu, (1960), p. 135.

7. Ch. Drouhet, *Vasile Alecsandri și scriitorii francezi* (1924) p. 229, asserts that of thirty-six one-act plays four are imitated from French. It would be truer to say that four (today, six) have known models. In any case the percentage of adaptations, is much higher with the comedies in more than one act; this proves that Alecsandri was able to construct a one-act play but did not enjoy doing longer plays.

8. Cf. Ch. Drouhet, *Vasile Alecsandri și scriitorii francezi,* p. 230.

9. Cf. as an example of what we mean by camouflage, in *Iorgu de la Sadagura:* "*Iorgu.* What is a land without canals, without commerce, without industry, without roads, without lib . . .? *Gîngu* (sneezing) Oh, I say!" Obviously the sneeze is a convenient device whereby the word "liberty," which would not have passed the censor, could be introduced without being uttered.

10. Cf. the autobiographical letter to Ubicini in V. Alecsandri, *Scrisori, Însemnări,* ed. M. Anineanu, p. 149: "I have had the happiness of waging

war on absurd and ingrained prejudices, of setting the Rumanian theater on its true national path and of proving that our language lends itself perfectly both to comedy and to music."

11. According to V. Alecsandri, *Poeziile,* ed. E. Rădulescu-Pogoneanu, I, pp. 222–23, the play dates from 1864; but it contains allusions to the peace between Prussia and Austria (1866) and to the withdrawal of the French expeditionary force from Mexico City (February, 1867).

12. Cf. D. Popovici, "*La double Échelle* de Planard şi *Scara Mîţei* de Alecsandri" in *Studii literare,* II.

13. Ch. Drouhet, *op. cit.,* pp. 148–58, notes several possible resemblances in detail to *La Comtesse d'Escarbagnac* and *Les Précieuses ridicules* of Moliere and to *Les Provinciaux à Paris* of L.-B. Picard; and, for the characterization of Chirita, to Madame Angot, a comic type created by Maillot in 1796 and frequently revived in the French theater.

14. E.g., at the start it is said that Bursuflescu's estate was bought "after the distribution of land," while Harţă goes on to assert that it was bought from the inheritance of Săftica's husband. Mariuca is in love with Harţă, who should be a man of about fifty, seeing that he himself says that for twenty years he has always been at law.

15. The review *Propăşirea* hastened to note it as the first Rumanian play. An official report of the French consul at Jassy refers to it as an important event and as a sign of change in the social mentality in Moldavia: this also indicates that it was a new departure.

16. This episode was later recounted as a characteristic expression of the "bonjourist" spirit of reform, in *Boieri şi ciocoi,* III, 2.

17. Cf. Ch. Drouhet, *Vasile Alecsandri şi scriitorii francezi,* p. 235.

18. Cf. the advice which he gave to Pantazi Ghica in a letter of November 18, 1865 (V. Alecsandri, *Corespondenţă,* ed. M. Anineanu [1960], p. 174): "Ayez surtout en vue que nous devons créer la véritable causerie en langue roumaine: la causerie fine, spirituelle, élégante, nuancée et originale."

19. It was published in *Convorbiri literare* of November 1, 1881; cf. Ch. Drouhet, *Vasile Alecsandri şi scriitorii francezi,* p. 192.

20. Cf. *ibid.,* p. 219: "We ought not to form our ideas of our peasants on the prose comedies of Alecsandri." But the same thing can be said of the aristocrat, the Greek, the Jew, and in general any character in Alecsandri's idealist theater.

21. G. Bogdan-Duică, *Vasile Alecsandri,* p. 15, quotes a letter of 1842 in which Alecsandri relates how the peasants beat an uncle of Kogălniceanu and how others, elsewhere, beat the Prince Cantacuzino—incidents which, in his opinion, "quite clearly prove a great stock of reason in the class of peasants." Alecsandri therefore was well aware that the reality was not very like his picture; on the other hand, there is a considerable measure of irony in the conclusion of his letter.

22. Cf. *Nunta țărănească* (*Teatru*, vol. II, p. 358): "It is good that the boyars should shake hands and be brothers with the peasants."

23. Cf., e.g., *Chirița în Iași* (*Teatru*, vol. II, p. 428).

24. In *Barbu Lăutarul* the character who turns the fiddler out of the house is referred to by the latter as *vătaf* (steward) and later as *ciocoi*. In *Boieri și ciocoi* the dress indicated for Lipicescu is "*ciocoi* clothes, but not livery."

25. In *Stan Covrigarul* the official is called in the text "a minor *ciocoi* from the Tribunal." Cf. the attacks on officials in *Ion Păpușarul, Paraponisitul,* and *Haimana*.

26. A character quoted in *Surugiul* has a right to the title of *cuconaș* and has a private Albanian guard of his own, and yet he is described as "one of those damned *ciocoi.*" In *Paracliserul*, Florin, a peasant who has received a considerable inheritance sings: "I too have become a *ciocoi.*" In *Boieri și ciocoi*, I, 7, all the boyars who have bought offices are called *ciocoi*.

27. It does not harmonize either with the victory won by the bourgeois over the aristocrat in *Ginerele lui Hagi Petcu* of with the situation of Radu in *Boieri și ciocoi*.

28. In *Agachi Flutur* Moisescu, a baptized Jew, talks Rumanian correctly, which is exceptional for Alecsandri's Jews; but "even though baptized, the Jew is still a moneylender" (I, 3: *Teatru*, vol. III, p. 685).

29. Cf. in *Lipitorile Satelor*, III, 7 (*Teatru*, vol. IV, p. 1453): "I have known decent Greeks, who honored their race and died for their country: I have known Captain Costea and Farmaki of the Hetairia with their comrades. These were men, these were Greeks with a heart." But generalizations are dangerous: even when he is talking of the Greeks in Greece, Alecsandri is far from favorable. Cf., e.g., a letter of 1889 in *Corespondență*, p. 206.

30. Cf. *Teatru*, vol. I, p. viii: "Our parents still preserve the simple customs of old time, ancestral beliefs and a patriarchal indulgence toward their subordinates; but the young masters, brought up under the rod of Greek teachers, are arrogant as parvenus."

31. Cf. *Iorgu de la Sadagura*, I, 4 (*Teatru*, vol. II, p. 919): "In those days every man with white hair was honored."

32. See the satire on Latinism in *Haimana, Clevetici,* and *Rusaliile*. It is curious that Alecsandri, who had a highly developed sense of language, uses in satire, and especially in *Rusaliile,* ill-chosen caricatures of Latinist formations and derivations—which fail in their purpose. *Capisci* (you understand) is not a Latinism but an Italianism; *florelinte* (flourishing is a hybrid Gallicism, from the French *florissant*. *Pășune* (passion), *espedat* (expedited), *să mă locomot* (to move myself) are clumsy inventions which reveal a total ignorance of genuine Latinism.

33. Cf. the examples quoted by Alexandrina Mititelu, "Considerazioni

intorno alla commedia romena prima di I. L. Caragiale" in *Societas Daco-Romana, Acta Philologica*, I (1958), 19–38.

34. *Gheşiţi* instead of *găsiţi; voişti* instead of *oişti.*

35. *Moţpănoi, viforoi, volintiroi, tîlheroi.*

36. *Vuăs (was); main got (mein Gott); ghevalt (Gewalt)*. All these are taken from *Herşcu Boccegiul.*

37. *Ginerele lui Hagi Petcu*, in *Teatrul*, vol. III, p. 1145.

38. In this comedy Alecsandri uses not merely words but whole phrases and indeed even a little dialogue in modern Greek; but they are common phrases from elementary instruction, which the poet still remembered. The verses quoted there are also part of schoolboy folklore.

39. Cf. I. Horia-Rădulescu, *Le Théâtre français dans les pays roumains* (Paris, 1965).

40. In *Rusaliile* (*Teatru*, vol. II, p. 915) confusion of *onomastică* and *mastic.*

41. Cf. *Kera Nastasia* (*Teatru*, vol. I, p. 72: *"Azi tare, mîine mare, poimîine pe spinare."* Verses in popular style about Vasilache Ţiganul in *Ion Păpuşarûl.*

42. Puns in *Haimana* on *permutat* and *prea mutat*, etc.

43. Cf. in *Iorgu de la Sadagura* (*Teatru*, vol. II, p. 915): "If I were not as silly as you, I should not be a poor boyar."

44. Of an unequal struggle: "Now he is on top, now I underneath."

45. "I have two nice children who are not in the least like me."

46. Poems in plays: *Măi Tătare, ţine-ţi calul* in *Nunta ţărănească, Român verde ca stejarul* in *Crai-Nou, Corona Moldovei* in *Cinel-cinel, Hora Unirii* in *Păcală şi Tîndală, Marşul ostaşilor români* in *Vivandiera, Cîntecul lui Ştefan cel Mare* in *Cetatea Neamţului, Barcarolă* (Cine 'n gondolă pe o noapte lină) in *Concina.*

47. Some of his gags were used by Caragiale. Cf. "I'm an educated youth . . . a grocer's apprentice" *(Kir Zuliaridis).* "If I haven't decorations, it's because they haven't given me any" *(Paraponisitul).* "I desire the convention to be respected, provided that it is totally changed" *(Clevetici).* The beginning of the comedy *Iaşii în Carnaval* was imitated by Caragiale in *Conu' Leonida faţă cu reacţiunea.* The story of the train journey in *Chiriţa în voiagiu* recalls *Domnul Goe.* In *Iaşii în carnaval* the part of the servant Safta inspired Brătescu-Voineşti's well-known sketch, *Metamorfoză.*

Chapter Seven

1. Charles Drouhet, *Vasile Alecsandri şi scriitorii francezi*, pp. 211–12.

2. The title recalls Goldoni's comedy *L'Avare Fastueux;* but the subject bears no resemblance, nor could Alecsandri have known the text of that comedy.

3. Alecsandri's biographers consider this date erroneous because in

the last act Lipicescu's forgery of a document is revealed by the fact that the watermark of the paper bore the date 1848: therefore the action of the last act is later than that date. Alecsandri's indications seem to be incomplete rather than erroneous in the sense that, in his conception, the action seems to extend over several years, before and after 1848.

4. Cf. Ch. Drouhet, *Vasile Alecsandri și scriitorii francezi,* pp. 265–67.

5. According to Drouhet, *op. cit.,* p. 266, it is a comedy of manners with traits of melodrama and farce:—a proof that it belongs to more than one genre. Elsewhere, pp. 238–39, Drouhet distinguishes social comedy from comedy of manners, and he places *Boieri și ciocoi* in the first category.

6. Cf. Al. Ciorănescu, *Teatrul românesc în versuri și izvoarele lui,* 1942.

7. Cf. *Despot Vodă,* preface, in which the author declares that imagination "finds it hard to return to the present day anthill of petty passions after meeting glorious princes and heroic Rumanians."

8. Cf. *ibid.:* "I was attracted by the *strange figure* of this prince and his *lightning passage* through Moldavian history. He was typical for me of those sixteenth-century adventurers, *half heroes, half bravoes* . . . For them *the fulfillment of their appetites* was all" (the italics are ours).

9. *Ibid.:* "an ambitious man drawn at first to a grand objective, but crushed by destiny."

10. Cf. *Despot-Vodă,* letter to A. Cantacuzino: "A series of historic tableaux intended together to form a whole, a *dramatic poem* or an *epic drama,* ad libitum."

11. Ch. Drouhet, *Vasile Alecsandri și scriitorii francezi,* pp. 270–88.

12. Cf., e.g., the first entrances of Limbă-Dulce (I, i), Despot (I, ii), Toroipan (I, 4), Ruxandra (I, ii, 1), Calabaican (I, ii, 3).

13. V. Alecsandri, *Scrisori, Însemnări,* ed. M. Anineanu, p. 30.

14. V. Alecsandri, *Poeziile,* ed. E. Radulescu-Pogoneanu, I, 297.

15. In *Convorbiri literare,* XII (1878–79), 186. For the name of the fountain Alecsandri adopted the less usual form *Blandusia* instead of *Bandusia.*

16. E.g., *libert* (I, iv), *cîmpii Olimpii* (I, viii), etc.

17. G. C. Nicolescu, *Viața lui Vasile Alecsandri,* pp. 621–24.

18. Alecsandri frequently alludes in his correspondence to the book which he used and which he calls *Les Amours d'Ovide.* Although this title is born by several French translations of the *Amores,* it is almost certain that the book referred to is *Les Amours d'Ovide,* translated by Mangeart and H. de Guerle with a study of Ovid by Jules Janin, published in Paris in 1883.

19. Cf. Ch. Drouhet, *Vasile Alecsandri și scriitorii francezi,* pp. 292–96.

20. V. Alecsandri, *Corespondență,* ed. M. Anineanu, p. 295.

Chapter Eight

1. Some examples of literal translation: "cînd sufletul său era lovit de vreun lucru" *(-lorsque son âme était frappée par quelque chose)*, "fără a muri niciodată" *(-sans jamais mourir)*. It is characteristic too that the name of the river Mugnone is transcribed, not from Italian as one might expect, but from French, *Miunione*.

2. E.g., "O vară de acele *unde* găinile fac ouă răscoapte" *(Haimana, in Teatru,* vol. I, p. 81); "ca *eu* nime nu-i trecător" *(ibid.,* p. 83). For other Gallicisms, which can be explained by misunderstandings of a French model, cf. Ch. Drouhet, *Vasile Alecsandri și scriitorii francezi,* p. 194.

3. This is rare and only in his first years of literary experiment. Thus in *O primblare la munți,* a judge is called a *Temisofiu* (son of Themis), a linguistic calque from Greek, which is perhaps ironic.

4. Thus *botega, granite, gelate.* Similarly in *O primblare la munți* the expression *salto mortale* is not an Italianizing affectation (as A. Marcu asserts in V. Alecsandri, *Proză,* ed. A. Marcu, p. 28), but a desperate measure, inasmuch as the Rumanian expression *salt mortal* and even the very word *salt* are of later date.

5. Even today the morphological connection of foreign names which do not fit Rumanian declensions is hard to fix: one usually says *Braziliei, Parisului,* and, less pleasingly, *Arno, Arnului;* but the oblique case of names like *Ines, Ajaccio,* still embarrasses the writer. In *Buchetiera de la Florența* Alecsandri has solved the problem by using the prefixed article *(a lui Arno).*

6. Cf. also A. Marcu, *Alecsandri și Italia* (1937), p. 37.

7. Alecsandri also published in *Propășirea* in 1844 the prose sketches *Călugărul și Pistolul* and *O intrigă la bal masché* and two essays in literary criticism.

8. According to G. Bogdan-Duică (cf. V. Alecsandri, *Proză,* ed. A. Marcu, p. 17), Alecsandri followed a German model; but cf., e.g., P.-A. Garnier, "Impressions de voyage d'une pièce de cinq sous" in *Revue de la Province,* IV (1843), pp. 125–41.

9. Alecsandri, *Teatru,* vol. I, p. viii.

Chapter Nine

1. Letter to C. Negri (1851), in V. Alecsandri, *Corespondență,* ed. M. Anineanu, p. 185.

2. Letter to C. Negri (1861), *ibid.,* p. 193.

Selected Bibliography

Manuscripts:

Many manuscripts of Alecsandri have been preserved in the different collections of the Rumanian Academy in Bucharest. His correspondence (2,150 letters) has been inventoried by Marta Anineanu, *Catalogul corespondenţei lui Vasile Alecsandri* (Bucharest, 1957). Many manuscripts (probably drafts or discarded versions, inasmuch as those in the collections of the Rumanian Academy are generally definitive versions) were lost in wartime (August, 1944) without having been studied or even inventoried.

Editions:

1. Complete Works
   Alecsandri himself published a collection, *Opere complete* (Bucharest, 1875–76), in eight volumes: four of plays, three of poems, and one of prose. The edition was published with particular care but naturally lacks the works written after 1876.

   A new complete edition, *Opere, ediţie critică îngrijită de G. C. Nicolescu,* has been announced, but so far only vol. I has been published (*Poezii: Doine, Lăcrămioare, Suvenire, Mărgăritărele* [Bucharest, 1965]). It is a useful edition, better than anything of the sort so far, but one in which the critical apparatus tends to smother the text proper.

2. Separate Works
   Poeziile populare, published by the author in 1852–53 (Jassy, 2 vols.), and in a definitive edition in 1866, have been republished with introduction and critical notes by G. Vrabie (Bucharest, 1965; 2 vols.).

   The volumes of poems (part II of *Opere complete* [Bucharest, 1875]) have frequently been reprinted. The text, and in particular the composition of the cycles, varies from one editor to another: Ion Bianu (Bucharest, 1896; 2 vols.) introduces changes, sometimes arbitrary; Gheorghe Adamescu (Bucharest, 1922) adds forgotten verses; Elena Rădulescu-Pogoneanu (Craiova, 1940; 2 vols.) gives a particularly careful text, but unfortunately anthological; it is completed by G. C. Nicolescu (Bucharest, 1955; 2 vols.).

   For the plays one may use *Comediile* in the edition of Al. Iordan (Craiova, 1933) and *Drama istorică* edited by G. Baiculescu (Craiova, 1937). There is a new edition by G. Orzea and F. I. Bociort (Bucharest, 1952–53; 2 vols.).

   Proză, edited by Al. Marcu (Craiova, 1930–33; 2 vols.), continues to be useful. For his correspondence *Scrisori,* published by I. Chendi and E. Carcalechi (Bucharest, 1904), have been completed by Marta Anineanu's two volumes, *Corespondență* (1960) and *Scrisori, Însemnări* (1964).

SECONDARY SOURCES

General Works:

BOGDAN, MARIE. *Autrefois et aujourd'hui.* Bucharest, 1929. Memories of the poet, written by his daughter.

BOGDAN-DUICĂ, G. *V. Alecsandri.* Bucharest, 1926. Commemorative publication with important biographical data.

CĂLINESCU, G. *V. Alecsandri.* Bucharest, 1965 (earlier in *Studii și cercetări de istorie literară,* VII, 1958) is almost the only purely literary investigation; it is often debatable.

NICOLESCU, G. C. *Viața lui V. Alecsandri.* Bucharest, 1961; rev. ed., 1965. A fundamental work, it does away with the need to consult most of the previous biographers but neglects the task of literary criticism.

PETRASCU, N. *V. Alecsandri.* Bucharest, 1894. First-rate biographical material. Republished in 1946.

ZAHARIA, N. *V. Alecsandri, viața și opera lui.* Bucharest, 1919. A compilation frequently outdated.

Special Studies:

CHRISTOPHOROV, P. "Un chapitre d'influences roumaines dans la poésie bulgare" in *Revue des Études Roumaines,* V–VI (1957–58), 95–126. On the influence of Alecsandri on the poetry of Ivan Vazov.

DROUHET, C. *V. Alecsandri și scriitorii francezi.* Bucharest, 1924. An important study for the literary bearings, especially where the plays are concerned.

MARCU, AL. *V. Alecsandri și Italia.* Bucharest, 1927. Biographical aspects and their reflection in the literary works.

PAPASTATE, C. D. *V. Alecsandri și Elena Negri.* Bucharest, 1947. Biographical study completed with the printing of the unpublished journal of the trip to Venice.

RAȘCU, I. M. *Eminescu și Alecsandri.* Bucharest, 1936. Study of Alecsandri's formative influence.

SCHWARZFELD, M. *Poeziile populare, colecția Alecsandri.* Jassy, 1889. *V. Alecsandri sau meșterul drege-strică.* Craiova, 1889. Violent attacks on the way in which the poet understood his obligations as a collector of folklore.

TAPPE, E. D. "Alecsandri and the English" in *Revue des Études Roumaines,* II (1954), 153–68.

Index